ALIVE

FROM THE

CENTER

ALIVE
FROM THE
CENTER

Earl Palmer

WORD BOOKS
PUBLISHER
WACO, TEXAS

ALIVE FROM THE CENTER

Library of Congress catalog card number: 81-70033
ISBN 0-8499-0122-7
Printed in the United States of America

To Lewis, Nancy, and Marian

There comes an hour in the afternoon when the child is tired of "pretending"; when he is weary of being a robber or a cowboy. It is then that he torments the cat.... The effect of this staleness is the same everywhere.... Right in the middle of all these things stands up an enormous exception. It is quite unlike anything else. It is a thing final like the trumpet of doom, though it is also a piece of good news, or news that seems too good to be true. It is nothing less than the loud assertion that this mysterious maker of the world has visited his world in Person.

Gilbert Keith Chesterton
from *The Everlasting Man*

CONTENTS

PREFACE

This book is about staying alive all of your life. It is about discovery and growing. It is a discipleship study in Paul's letters to the people he loved at Corinth. What I am offering is not a paragraph-by-paragraph commentary on the Corinthian letters. Instead, I have looked at these letters in a special way.

I have considered Paul's correspondence from the standpoint of one single issue. It is the issue that Paul himself raises at the very beginning of his first letter. That issue may be stated either in positive or negative terms. Positively, it is the question of convergence, that is, what is it that deserves to be at the center in the life of a person or a people? Negatively put, it is the problem of adriftness or imbalance. This happens when a person or group of people either fail to find the true center for their lives, or having once found it in the morning of their lives they then drift off-center later in the day. There are other great and vital themes within 1 and 2 Corinthians. But I believe the issue of keeping on center is the most consistent thread throughout the letters, and I offer this special and narrowly focused study because I believe this issue is as urgent for our generation as it was for Corinth.

Paul is brilliant in these letters as he takes hold of both the positive and the negative implications of the question of finding a center. He is sensitive to the ambiguities and the crosscurrent of competing claims and counterclaims that confront every human being who is seeking to discover the true center for life. Paul is always bold and definite; he is also warm and human. I commend the Corinthian correspondence to anyone who is searching for the true center of life. I commend these letters to anyone who has found the going very hard in the afternoon of life and has even been tempted toward options that drain away the joy and spontaneity and belovedness of the morning. I hope that these theological reflections of mine will be a help for you in your own journey both toward and within convergence.

I am personally very grateful to the many people of all ages who have been helpful to me as I have drawn together these studies. I want to thank my staff colleagues, the fellowship groups, and the congregation of First Presbyterian Church of Berkeley, who have played such a key enabling role in my life as a Christian, a pastor, and a teacher. There are so many others. I especially remember the life-changing week-long conference with young pastors and youth workers in South Africa (South Africa Youth Ministry Assembly), where I shared these studies. Most of all I thank God for my wife, Shirley, and for our children, Anne, Jonathan, and Elizabeth, for their encouragement all day long.

Earl Palmer
Berkeley, California 1981

INTRODUCTION

Two summers ago my children surprised me with a gift; it was an original cassette recording of a Bud Abbott/Lou Costello radio show of 1946. I am sure that I had heard that show at its first appearance, since radio shows and the movies were very big events in my youthful years. We have listened to the cassette several times; Abbott and Costello are still funny even after thirty-five years, and their sketch "Who's on First," which appeared in this 1946 show, is a classic. But to my amazement all of us, and especially my children, found the commercials as funny as the comedians!

I was so impressed by this fact that I asked my daughter, Anne, to write out an exact transcript of the commercials as they appeared on that 1946 one-hour show. I will now replay them for you. Five different male voices and one female voice were involved in the various sequences. A chorus and full orchestra sang out the opening and closing signals. The show that evening began as follows:

C—AM—EL—S.
That's right, folks!
C for comedy,
A for Abbott,
M for Maxwell,
E for Ennis,
L for Lou Costello.
Put them all together and they spell Camel!

Experience is the best teacher. Try a Camel; let your own experience tell you why more people are smoking Camels than ever before, and draw up a chair for tonight's Camel show starring Bud Abbott and Lou Costello.

*   *   *   *   *

Experience is the *best* teacher.

It happened shortly after the end of the war. Two cigarettes glow in the dusk on the veranda of a country house as a man and woman are chatting. The woman remarks, "Robert, you've changed your cigarette brand. This is a *Camel*. I can tell without even looking."

"Yes, I *have* changed my brand. You know how we smoked whatever cigarettes we could get during the war?"

"Don't I!"

"Yes, I must have tried all the brands during that shortage. That's when I found I liked Camels best."

"And weren't you *right*!"

Yes, experience *is* the best teacher! During the wartime shortage, people smoked whatever cigarettes they could get. It was this experience that taught millions the *differences* in cigarette quality. As smokers tried cigarette after cigarette on their *T zone* (that's *T* for *taste* and *T* for *throat*), it was Camel's rich full flavor and cool mildness that stood out from all the others. The result: (different taped voice) "Today more people smoke Camels than ever before."

Experience is the best teacher. Try a Camel. And while you light up a Camel here's Skinny Ennis with "Linda" . . .

*   *   *   *   *

(official voice) According to a recent nationwide survey, more *doctors* smoke Camels than any other cigarette.

Three leading independent research organizations·asked this question of 113,597 doctors: "What cigarette do you smoke, Doctor?" The brand named most was Camel. Now you probably enjoy rich full flavor and cool mildness in a cigarette just as much as doctors do, and that's why if you're not a Camel smoker now, try a Camel on *your T zone*, (that's *T* for *taste* and *T* for *throat*), your true proving ground for any cigarette. See if Camel's rich flavor of superbly blended choice tobaccos isn't extra delightful to your taste. See if Camel's cool mildness isn't in harmony with your throat. See if you too don't say, "Camels suit my T zone to a tee."

* * * * *

During the war the makers of Camel cigarettes sent a total of over one hundred fifty million free Camels to our fighting men overseas. Now free Camels are sent to servicemen's hospitals instead. This week the Camels go to: Veteran's Hospital, Fort Lion, Colorado, U.S.A.F. Station Monson Field, Tucson, Arizona, U.S. Naval Hospital, Quanticol, Virginia, U.S. Marine Hospital, Baltimore, Maryland, and Veteran's Hospital, Palo Alto, California.

* * * * *

Camel broadcasts go out to the United States three times a week, and we broadcast to practically every area in the world where our men are still stationed and to our good neighbors in Central and South America.

* * * * *

Prince Albert.

Prince Albert, pipe appeal, they're one and the same thing. Any tobacco burns, makes smoke, but where else can you have the tobacco that has the pipe appeal of Prince Albert, the coolness, mildness, the rich, full flavor? Prince Albert is specially treated to insure against tongue bite. Cut to smoke slow and cool. So pack your pipe with mellow, rich Prince Albert. Enjoy pipe appeal with Prince Albert.

* * * * *

Be sure to tune in again next week for another great Abbott and Costello show brought to you by Camel cigarettes. And remember, experience is the best teacher. Try a Camel; let your own experience tell you why more people are smoking Camels than ever before.

C—AM—EL—S

This is Michael Roy Holiday wishing you all a pleasant goodnight for Camel.

What an ad! So friendly! So full of life! So much interesting data! So UNTRUE! My children were astounded by the ad, especially by the "T zone" encouragement and the "doc-tors" survey. Apart from "Who's on First," the ads were for us the funniest part of the show. But they also make me stop and think, and it makes me not a little uneasy to think that when the show was first aired in 1946 we who listened by our radios were not laughing at the survey or the "T zone" advocacy. We were convinced! We took up smoking.

This experience forces me to ask a question of myself and of my generation today. What about the values and persuasive advocacies that we buy into and adopt and believe today? How will they stand thirty-five years of testing? On some lazy day thirty-five years from now, will our children and their children be laughing at the current relevancies of our life today?

Or let me put the question in positive terms. How do I find the values and reasons and meanings for life today that will last for thirty-five years and stay as fresh in that afternoon of my life as they were in the morning of my life? This is the inescapable question that every human being must ask, because there comes a time in the afternoon when a child grows tired playing cowboys and rob-bers... "it is then that he torments the cat."

The problem is that the values and truths that we were once so certain of have a way of wearing out on us; they go stale in the afternoon. When this happens to us, every-thing and everyone around us suffers—even ourselves, even the cat!

I think it is correct, as Chesterton warns, that staleness in the afternoon is the cause of our most harmful sins and our most nightmarish fears. For example, the sin of adul-tery is worse than the sin of fornication. Fornication is the sin of youthful desire, the result of the carelessness of the high-energy passion of unmarried youth. It is a "hot" sin and it does harm, but adultery is a "cold" sin and it does even more harm. It is the sin of a married man or woman who has grown stale and now breaks the commitments that were made for a lifetime, who wanders away not because the energy level is alive and fresh, but because the afternoon has taken its toll and spiritual-emotional-physical fatigue has set in. "It commonly happens in periods of disillusionment like our own, when philosophies are bankrupt and life appears without hope—men and women may turn to lust in sheer boredom..."[1]

C. S. Lewis puts it plainly in the toast of Screwtape in which Screwtape complains about the quality of sinners: "Then there was the Lukewarm Casserole of Adulterers. Could you find in it any trace of a fully inflamed, defiant, rebellious, insatiable lust? I couldn't. They all tasted to me like undersexed morons who had blundered or trickled into the wrong beds in automatic response to sexy advertisements, or to make themselves feel modern and emancipated, ... or even because they had nothing else to do."[2] What happens is that the joy of the morning can run out in the afternoon and a staleness, a resourcelessness can take over.

The sins of pornography are of the same origin—not an exuberant, careless embrace of life, but rather the cynical and jaded attempt to shock our senses awake and to snap ourselves out of oppressive boredom. So also is the case of the deadly sin of pride, with its desperate attempt to prop up and defend a hollow man who stands alone and frightened at the latter part of the day. The fascination with exotic religious movements is almost always the result of spiritual disillusionment and fatigue.

How shall we stay alive and fresh throughout the day? First of all, we need to find in the morning the TRUTH that we can make the center of our lives—the truth that lasts because its own integrity and inner durability is able to withstand the pressure of time. Secondly, we ourselves need to grow in our relationship to that all-day truth. Every man and woman has the privilege of the journey from morning to evening. There are new mornings that by surprise come into our lives—new chances, the occasions of freedom, the crisis moments when a major choice confronts us. These morning events are the stuff that makes up the mystery of who we are as human beings. How we choose and whether we choose and what we do with the morning events will profoundly shape the journey of the day.

It is a fact that the whole created order suffers from the "stale in the afternoon" person. But it is even more permanently true that the world benefits when a man or woman stays fresh and alive, renewed and growing throughout the day, secure in the center of his or her being. When a person knows and experiences the joyous liberation of belovedness, the results are nourishing to the people around him. Hope spreads like the lights of a city settled upon a hill.

This book is about the discovery of that belovedness and its holy origin. This book is about the all-day durability of that morning breakthrough, about the true Center of all things. Everyone benefits, even the cat.

1.

CONVERGENCE

In 1978, I met the American mountaineer Willy Unisold. It was some eight months before the tragic climbing accident on Mt. Rainier that took his life. One of my own interests from the time of my youth has been mountaineering, and I was fascinated to hear him tell of his experiences in the successful ascent of the west ridge of Mt. Everest, as well as other expeditions. At one point, he turned the dialogue around and asked the group at our table a question: "Why do you think people climb mountains?" I spoke up with the famous reply of another mountaineer, Sir George Mallory, who when asked why he climbed the Matterhorn, answered, "Because it is there!" Willy Unisold was well aware of Mallory's answer, but he told our group that he was not satisfied with it. Mr. Unisold suggested a deeper reason. He said, "People climb mountains because of a universal desire to find the point of convergence." The most dramatic moment in mountaineering is just that experience of physical convergence in time and space and geography that a climber feels when he or she finally stands at the true summit of a mountain. Everything is there. All of the lines come together; every sharp face, every impossible ridge, every

19

glaciated landscape is somehow resolved and fulfilled in one outcropping of rock or ice just beneath his feet. Finally, the whole makes sense to the climber's eye and mind and feelings. He is able to relate to the vastness of river systems and the jumble of glacial moraines of the sheer face of rock and the welcoming forests at the timberline. It is not that the personal self is any larger for being there; in fact, an inevitable and dangerous vulnerability surrounds the moment. Nevertheless, there is the shout of exhilaration and triumph. With such a central vantage point, everything comes together!

The yearning for convergence is a human desire that not only expresses itself toward small and great mountains but also has its analogy in every other realm of life. The human personality has an inclination toward finding center points from which the whole of life might come into scale and focus. We were made "to live from the center," to use Dietrich Bonhoeffer's phrase, and it is from the center that the complexity of the whole of life can be grasped and made sense of.

During these last forty years, we have been living in the convergence era of science. From the time of Albert Einstein's discovery of the high-speed expansion of the universe, the whole of the scientific community has been tracing down the convergent lines with probes into deep space that give us clues about events in the primeval past of this vast and expanding universe. Radio-telescope astronomers have now interpreted the bombardment of static which surrounds our planet in wave upon wave as the reverberation of an original "big bang"—the convergent point when at one instant light and gravity and mass and energy were begun. The convergent instinct that has long intrigued philosophers from Aristotle to Blaise Pascal to Rudolf Otto has now become the instinct of physics as well.

St. Augustine began his own confessions with these

words, "The heart is restless until it finds its rest in Thee."
His words express a longing for what I believe to be the
one true center, the convergence point of all history—
Jesus Christ. I want this book to be a book about that true
center, but also about the forest edges and the sometimes
steep, sometimes hazardous ridges, the valleys, streams,
lakes, the sudden outcroppings and dropoffs, the ener-
getic and the quiet stretches that all combine to make up
what we experience as our lives and, taken together, as
existence itself.

There are many convergence parables within life—the
mountaintop experience we have been discussing is one.
For example, the wheel is a convergence analogy, with the
spokes converging into a single central hub. Most of the
athletic games we play are convergence games in which all
the factors move in toward one single score and conclusion. Jesus Christ told convergence parables. The parable
of the prodigal son is a convergence story in which each
event and person within the story is finally understood in
the context of the central event—the two sons' encounter
with the father's love and authority. The parable of the
good Samaritan is also a convergence parable in which the
storyteller draws each character within the story toward a
convergence at the place of grave human crisis. When
Paul, the apostle to the world, tells his parable of the
church and likens the church to a body, that example is a
convergence metaphor; each separate member is related to
the body as a whole, with Christ as head. Another example of convergence is the building image in Ephesians,
with the person of Christ as the cornerstone of a structure.

The life and ministry of Jesus Christ is also a convergence narrative. And the most profound convergence
of all time occurs as Jesus radically intersects the very line
of history itself by his death and resurrection—the radical
interruption at history's center.

Every human story is in its final telling the story of convergence. Every human life has as its chief quest the quest for true center. Happiness and despair, friendship and want, adventure and aloneness are the raw, unfinished materials that make up the valleys and steep, narrow passes of that human journey. The center point, the point of convergence, is the point from which the whole makes sense.

If human beings are to make any sense to us, they must be seen and studied in the context of the universal quest for convergence of which our games and jokes, and religious and folk stories, and fears and dreams, and now even our astrophysics are symbols. We men and women do foolish and strange things to find the center. But a necessary critique of the inadequacy of the search ought not to dismiss the search itself!

There is in all fairy tales the presence of what J. R. R. Tolkien calls "eucatastrophy," the *good catastrophy*, the arrival of the decisive crisis moment, "the sudden joyous turn." It is another name for the convergence point of the story, the moment which makes the entire story clear. These stories are important to us in childhood and adulthood because they prepare us emotionally and spiritually for the profound good catastrophy that in ultimate reality is the Alpha and Omega point of existence.

This also is the importance of adventures that happen in our lives. Children need, in proportion to their perception, adventure stories, and they need adventure experiences as they grow up in order to prepare them for the larger convergence experiences of life. I agree, on the basis of my own pastoral experience in Berkeley, with Professor Bruno Bettelheim in his conclusion that most young men and women who have moved into drug culture are individuals who entered the critical teenage years already lonely and starved for good adventure stories and concrete adventure experiences of their own. The promise through mind-altering chemicals makes sense to them, whether LSD, alcohol, cocaine, or marijuana. The choice for a high point through drugs is a faulty choice, and the catastrophy that they produce is not a good one, as the human brain is assaulted and tampered with and confused by drugs. But the search was the right search.

The search is the adventure; and just as it is in every adventure, the good catastrophy is the surprise that happens when the convergence point finds the searcher.

2.

A VISIT TO CORINTH

"Not everyone can afford a trip to Corinth." The seaport of Corinth at the midpoint of the first century was second only to Rome in wealth and importance within the Empire. It had not always been so. In the time of ancient Greece, Corinth had been an illustrious and splendid city built on a grand scale, but in the year 146 B.C. the Romans had ravaged the city and destroyed its temples. One hundred years later, in 46 B.C., the Roman Emperor Julius Caesar had reestablished Corinth and begun a restoration that soon brought the city back to its former outward glory. Because of the Mediterranean Sea trade routes and the strategic location of the city on a narrow strip of land between the Aegean Sea and the Gulf of Corinth, which opened into the Adriatic Sea, Corinth benefited from all trade coming to and from the Eastern Mediterranean and Rome. Ships would put in with cargo that was then transferred overland from one sea to the other. The Emperor Nero realized the importance of this location and instituted construction of an ambitious engineering project— the Corinthian Canal—which was finally completed centuries later in 1898. The city was physically impressive in the first century, with its 1800-foot-high citadel crowned with the temple to Aphrodite.

It was to this city that Paul came after his visit to Athens, and in this place a first-century Christian church was founded. Luke tells us of this founding:

> After this he left Athens and went to Corinth. And he found a Jew named Aquila, a native of Pontus, lately come from Italy with his wife Priscilla, because Claudius had commanded all the Jews to leave Rome. And he went to see them; and because he was of the same trade he stayed with them, and they worked, for by trade they were tentmakers. And he argued in the synagogue every sabbath, and persuaded Jews and Greeks (Acts 18:1–4).

Does it seem odd to you that the people who lived in a city like Corinth should become Christians? They don't seem to have been the type! The contrasts between them and Paul's group of Christians were strong and striking. The Corinthians were lavish and excessive. The Hellenistic scholar Lightfoot estimated that there were four hundred thousand slaves in Corinth at the time of Paul's visit. These slaves were the human underpinning for the transportation industry and the luxurious lifestyle of the Roman citizens who lived in and visited Corinth. The temples of Aphrodite were like a vast brothel system which involved the sexual exploitation of thousands of temple slaves. Into this atmosphere had come Paul and his friends Priscilla and Aquila, Apollos, Silvanus, Timothy and Luke. In contrast to that of the citizenry of Corinth, their message and lifestyle were spare and simple. Later, when Paul wrote to the Corinthians, he reminded them of this simplicity:

> When I came to you, brethren, I did not come proclaiming to you the testimony of God in lofty words or wisdom. For I decided to know nothing among you except Jesus Christ

and him crucified. And I was with you in weakness and in
much fear and trembling; and my speech and my message
were not in plausible words of wisdom, but in demonstra-
tion of the Spirit and of power, that your faith might not
rest in the wisdom of men but in the power of God (1 Cor.
2:1-5).

But what is fascinating is that what Paul said and the way
he lived made sense to large numbers of people in
Corinth. Many people in this city believed in the gospel of
Jesus Christ, and the church was established at Corinth.

There are other contrasts too. When it came to the world
of philosophy and ideas, the Corinthians had a trading-
city intellectualism. They jumped from fad to fad; their
reputation as a carefree city had long been recognized in
Greek drama, where Corinthians were usually portrayed
as shiftless and as drunkards. In contrast to this Corinthian style of life, what they heard from Paul was marked
by a total honesty and transparent concern for truth.

Therefore, having this ministry by the mercy of God, we do
not lose heart. We have renounced disgraceful, under-
handed ways; we refuse to practice cunning or to tamper
with God's word, but by the open statement of the truth we
would commend ourselves to every man's conscience in the
sight of God (2 Cor. 4:1-2).

This forthright message was so unlike their usual
ideological fadism. The fact is that this earnest message
won many Corinthians to embrace Jesus Christ as the
truth.

The Corinthians were opportunistic. They had taken
advantage of their ideal location to exact a high price for
every ship that put in to their seaport. In order to avoid the
treacherous storms of the Aegean Sea, the shippers had to
pay dearly for the safety of Corinth's transit. The Roman
institution of human slavery provided for Corinth the

manpower to move cargo from one sea to the other. This city was reaping bountifully where it had not sown. Against this order of economic and social injustice, Paul called out to the Corinthians to become disciples and ambassadors of a new order founded not upon exploitation but upon the way of sacrifice and generosity:

> But we have this treasure in earthen vessels, to show that the transcendent power belongs to God and not to us. We are afflicted in every way, but not crushed; perplexed, but not driven to despair; persecuted, but not forsaken; struck down, but not destroyed; always carrying in the body the death of Jesus, so that the life of Jesus may also be manifested in our bodies. For while we live we are always being given up to death for Jesus' sake, so that the life of Jesus may be manifested in our mortal flesh. So death is at work in us, but life in you (2 Cor. 4:7–12).

> Under the test of this service, you will glorify God by your obedience in acknowledging the gospel of Christ, and by the generosity of your contribution for them and for all others; while they long for you and pray for you, because of the surpassing grace of God in you. Thanks be to God for his inexpressible gift! (2 Cor. 9:13–15).

The question is, "Why should people like the Corinthians become Christians?" They don't seem to fit with either the content or the inner style of the gospel message. Paul reminds the Corinthians of this essential incongruity in his first letter: "You did not become Christians because of the human reasons and standards of your own cultural setting" (1 Cor. 1:26, my paraphrase). That is the point! When they decided upon the gospel, they chose a convergence point for their lives that gave no resemblance to the lower reaches of their Corinthian value system. Theirs was a city which luxuriated in the wreckage of human life and depended upon brutality and interpersonal hurtfulness. Now a new and breathtaking discovery had broken in upon this decadence.

How did it happen? The answer to that question is that Paul had managed to point the Corinthians to the very center and soul of Christianity—Jesus Christ the Lord. It is that living center that won them. Paul himself puts it this way:

> For consider your call, brethren; not many of you were wise according to worldly standards, not many were powerful, not many were of noble birth; but God chose what is foolish in the world to shame the wise, God chose what is weak in the world to shame the strong, God chose what is low and despised in the world, even things that are not, to bring to nothing things that are, so that no human being might boast in the presence of God. He is the source of your life in Christ Jesus, whom God made our wisdom, our righteousness and sanctification and redemption; therefore, as it is written, "Let him who boasts, boast of the Lord" (1 Cor. 1:26-31—also see 1 Cor. 2:1-5).

In other words, when these Corinthians listened to Paul, they were able to see the new *authority* and *lordship* of Jesus Christ over against the old *wealth* and *forms of power* that they had once obeyed as strong.

This new power was a surprise to those who had known the old power and the old wealth. It was higher, and it was richer, than the Mediterranean villas and the luxury of an empire gone indulgent and consumptive. Jesus Christ had the power to change life, to forgive sin, to heal brokenness, to conquer despair, to set people free, to give life in the place of death! This is the good news that startled the Corinthians by its very understatement and "down-to-earthness." This was worthy of being at the center of their lives. The authority of Jesus, not Paul nor his eloquent friend Apollos, won the Corinthians.

Jesus Christ won their respect intellectually, too. They

saw in Jesus Christ the truth, the profound *wisdom* that is able to integrate the parts of life and give meaning to the whole. This is something neither the city gods nor the powerful and skillfully ordered Roman world were able to do. From this center, this Alpha-Omega point, this mountain summit, the Corinthians were able to see the whole of existence, and the parts now made sense, whereas before the view from different angles seemed contradictory and confusing.

But more than gaining an integrated view of life, they discovered the love of God. It was not love as an ideological concept but as the personal event—Jesus Christ the person and "him crucified" in behalf of the human family. The Corinthians discovered the loving and caring center of all being, and that center is Jesus Christ himself. This is the theological force of Paul's opening reminder to the Corinthians in his first letter. The heart of the Christian faith is its living Lord. It is his *authority*, his *truth*, his *event love* that forms the center of Christianity.

Paul describes this grand convergence by the use of many examples. In his letter to the Ephesians, he makes use of the imagery of a building and calls Jesus Christ the chief cornerstone of that building. In Paul's letter to the Romans and in 2 Corinthians, Paul uses the image of the body to describe the central relationship of Jesus Christ to those who will trust in him. If Paul had conceived of a twentieth-century image, it seems to me he might have thought of a wheel as a parable of the relationships of those who trust in Christ. In this case, Jesus Christ would be the strong center hub of the wheel.

What happened at Corinth is that Jesus Christ drew men and women, young and old, to himself from every part of their first-century social context. We have clear evidence from the letters of 1 and 2 Corinthians of the rich mixture of peoples that made up the Corinthian church. He loved them; he made sense to them; he won them—Jews,

Greeks, Romans, the poor, the rich, Roman citizens, Roman slaves. Each of these persons brought to the center unique aspirations, yearnings, hurts, needs, interests. Yet, they all had one fact in common. Each was won to the center by the Center. In one way or another, Jesus Christ became real and personally known to them. The Holy Spirit assured this broad collection of people—and each one in a way different than the next—of the reality of the love of Jesus Christ.

This is how it happened in the first century at places like Corinth, Philippi, Rome, Jerusalem. This is how it still happens in places like San Francisco, London, Nairobi and Hong Kong. By surprise and often in the most unlikely places and settings, people discover the claims of the Gospel of Jesus Christ. They personally discover that the Lord of that claim is relevant and makes sense to them in terms of their own journey and quest. When we modern-day Corinthians look around and see who else has been drawn to the Center, we are in our own century as amazed by the kinds of people and the places from which they have all come as were the people of the Corinth of the first century.

My purpose in this study will now be to try to understand what happens to the man or woman who discovers that living convergence point: ". . . yet for us there is one God, the Father, from whom are all things and for whom we exist, and one Lord, Jesus Christ, through whom are all things and through whom we exist" (1 Cor. 8:6).

3.

A TWENTIETH-CENTURY
PARABLE

Imagine the front wheel of a bicycle made up of hub, spokes, rim—three essential parts. Each part is very different from the other; yet taken together, the wheel is able to carry weight, absorb sudden road shock, and in tandem with the power drive of the back wheel is able to transfer the biker's energy to forward motion so that the whole assembly is an efficient marvel of engineering.

I am thinking of this wheel as a convergence parable about life and at the same time—especially in this chapter—as a parable about each of us as separate human beings. At this point, let me explore by means of this parable one question: If I were to choose Jesus Christ as the center, the hub of my life, what then are the different kinds or sets of spokes that will make up my life?

It seems to me that there are four main groups or sets of spokes. In this chapter, let us look closely at the first set.

First of all, there are two primary spokes. I will describe them as two realities about myself that I discover in finding the true hub. These spokes at first glance appear as opposites, but in fact they really work antiphonally to balance each other. The one is the discovery I make of my sinfulness; the other is the discovery I make of my belovedness. In the biblical view of personhood, these two spokes always go together.

When Saul of Tarsus met Jesus Christ as the Lord and true center on the road to Damascus, he then saw more clearly than ever before the false centers that had held sway up to that point in his life. "Saul, Saul, why do you persecute me? It hurts you to kick against the goads" (Acts 26:14). This roadway event cleared the air for Paul. It was one decisive part of a process that had begun years earlier, with his early training in the law, his student years under the teacher Gamaliel, and later during his angry opposition toward the early Christians. The process reached a crisis point on the Damascus Road and later at the house of Judas, and it continued on into the successive passages of his life. Paul was learning throughout this journey about who the Lord Jesus Christ is, and he was also learning about himself.

That which Paul learned about himself was disquieting to him; he never forgot the alarming discovery he made about himself at the same moment he was discovering the worthiness and love of Jesus Christ. His experience was much like the experience the prophet Isaiah tells us of in Isaiah 6: "In the year that King Uzziah died I saw the Lord...."

Isaiah's first overwhelming feeling when he met the Lord in this vision was the feeling of his own sinfulness:

And I said: "Woe is me! For I am lost; for I am a man of unclean lips, and I dwell in the midst of a people of unclean lips; for my eyes have seen the King, the Lord of hosts!" (Isa. 6:5).

But the alarm Isaiah felt was matched by the dramatic discovery of forgiveness:

Then flew one of the seraphim to me, having in his hand a burning coal which he had taken with tongs from the altar.

And he touched my mouth, and said: "Behold, this has
touched your lips; your guilt is taken away, and your sin is
forgiven" (Isa. 6:6–7).

This twofold discovery the prophet Isaiah and Saul the
Pharisee made is the realization of the two spokes that
become a permanent part of the wheel of every Christian's
life. The downward one is the sinfulness spoke. It is the
profound and disturbing probe of the light of truth into
our lives. The upward spoke exists in dramatic tension to
this downward one, and provides the antiphonal balance.
It is the belovedness spoke, the discovery that we are
loved by God for who we really are. We need the first
spoke, and we need the second spoke. Both shall be a part
of the wheel of our lives; as Dietrich Bonhoeffer said, "You
cannot hear the last word until you have heard the next to
the last."[1] The sinfulness realization is a prior doorway or
outer gate which opens up to the surprising and grand
inner doorway of grace and joy; but both doorways are
essential to the house, just as both spokes are necessary to
the wheel.

Moreover, the sinfulness spoke is not eliminated by the
discovery of belovedness. It stays! On the other hand, the
realistic law and gospel disclosure of my moral and
spiritual frailty does not destroy me because it is matched
by the sheer grace of the God who really knows who I am
and still loves me. This grace is not the "cheap grace" that
denies the presence of sin—no "justification of sin," as
Bonhoeffer warns us. Rather, it is a grace that has truth at
its heart and that confers upon my life a belovedness that
is based not on my innocence or my excellence but on my
redemption in Christ—the "justification of the sinner":

Cheap grace means grace as a doctrine, a principle, a system. It means forgiveness of sins proclaimed as a general
truth, the love of God taught as the Christian 'conception'
of God. An intellectual assent to that idea is held to be of

itself sufficient to secure remission of sins. The Church
which holds the correct doctrine of grace has, it is supposed, *ipso facto* a part in that grace. In such a Church the
world finds a cheap covering for its sins; no contrition is
required, still less any real desire to be delivered from sin.
Cheap grace therefore amounts to a denial of the living
Word of God, in fact, a denial of the Incarnation of the
Word of God.

Cheap grace means the justification of sin without the
justification of the sinner.[2]

These two spokes accompany me all my life, and they
each have a part to play in keeping me whole and balanced. Because of the one spoke, I know of the profound
complexity of my needs, and I am reminded by its presence that there will never be a time during my life when I
am released of that complexity. It is part of what being
human means, and to the last day of my life, I will need
the healing and forgiving grace of God.

The prayer in the Roman Catholic sacrament of extreme
unction expresses this basic human need very well: "Lord
Jesus, have mercy upon me." This is the earnest recognition that, whether we are a bishop in the church or a
condemned felon under sentence, we need to say the
same prayer—because of what our humanity means. Our
humanity and the freedom that goes with that humanity is
not taken away from us when we are forgiven. The sinfulness spoke, though it may embarrass and confound our
idealistic notions of human greatness, is a very important
spoke.

Most idealistic models of human personality and personhood aspire toward self-perceived flawlessness. They
picture mankind as having no needs that cannot be provided from within. This kind of self-perception becomes
dangerous when a leader of a political or religious movement claims flawlessness for himself or herself. Such a
person leads others on the basis of the resources of a

"pure" inner self; and, having no awareness of moral weakness, that kind of a leader will not welcome the check and balance of either law or gospel.

The twentieth century has given us many such idealized leadership models, and we have suffered deeply because of them. These persons place themselves above all inquiry into motives or actions. They insist upon their right to stand above practical check and balance, because they do not have any real consciousness of their limitations. The inevitable drift of this personality type is toward tyranny and finally despair, because it is a self-understanding founded upon a fallacy, upon a misunderstanding of what it is to be a human being.

The people who perceive themselves as innocent and who, therefore, have no consciousness of the ambiguities of being human are usually the people who inflict the most harm on other people around them. They do not know how to ask forgiveness, because they have no real acknowledgment of the possibility of their own wrongdoing. Therefore, they go through life unhealed, isolated, and—finally—stale in the afternoon. They blame others for the harm that happens around them. But what is worst of all, they do not ever really enjoy the discovery of being loved. Their self-understanding has wrongly taught them that the affection they receive comes because they have earned it. They have settled for admiration in the place of love, and that is a very poor exchange.

We human beings spend a great amount of our time in the quest for admiration. Admiration is a quality that deserves some consideration at this point; it is important and should not be either rejected or carelessly rebuked. Admiration is the reward for achievement, and it has an important role to play in the total mixture of human motivations. I believe that the desire for admiration, for the kind of respect that comes from a task well done, is a sign of spiritual and emotional health. It is Jesus himself who teaches this to us in the stewardship/kingdom parables: "Well done, good and faithful servant; you have been faithful over a little, I will set you over much" (Matt. 25:21). Paul shares openly and boldly with his Corinthian readers the accounts of his own trials, his spiritual break-throughs and of heroic achievements, so that the Corinthians will recognize and admire him for deeds about which they were evidently unaware or had failed to recognize. Paul is completely forthright. He does not play either emotional or spiritual games with them. He wants their respect, and he comes straight to the point about the matter and tells them so.

Paul does not need courses in assertiveness training, as the texts of 1 and 2 Corinthians clearly demonstrate. Note some of these texts:

> But we will not boast beyond limit, but will keep to the limits God has apportioned us, to reach even to you. For we are not overextending ourselves, as though we did not reach you; we were the first to come all the way to you with the gospel of Christ. We do not boast beyond limit, in other men's labors; but our hope is that as your faith increases, our field among you may be greatly enlarged, so that we may preach the gospel in lands beyond you, without boast-ing of work already done in another's field. "Let him who boasts, boast of the Lord" (2 Cor. 10:13–17).

> But whatever any one dares to boast of—I am speaking as a fool—I also dare to boast of that. Are they Hebrews? So am I. Are they Israelites? So am I. Are they descendants of Abraham? So am I. Are they servants of Christ? I am a better one—I am talking like a madman—with far greater labors, far more imprisonments, with countless beatings, and often near death. Five times I have received at the hands of the Jews the forty lashes less one. Three times I have been beaten with rods; once I was stoned. Three times I have been shipwrecked; a night and a day I have been adrift at sea; on frequent journeys, in danger from rivers, danger from robbers, danger from my own people, danger

from Gentiles, danger in the city, danger in the wilderness, danger at sea, danger from false brethren; in toil and hardship, through many a sleepless night, in hunger and thirst, often without food, in cold and exposure. And, apart from other things, there is the daily pressure upon me of my anxiety for all the churches. Who is weak, and I am not weak? Who is made to fall, and I am not indignant? If I must boast, I will boast of the things that show my weakness. The God and Father of the Lord Jesus, he who is blessed for ever, knows that I do not lie. At Damascus, the governor under King Aretas guarded the city of Damascus in order to seize me, but I was let down in a basket through a window in the wall, and escaped his hands. I must boast; there is nothing to be gained by it, but I will go on to visions and revelations of the Lord. I know a man in Christ who fourteen years ago was caught up to the third heaven—whether in the body or out of the body I do not know, God knows. And I know that this man was caught up into Paradise— whether in the body or out of the body I do not know, God knows—and he heard things that cannot be told, which man may not utter. On behalf of this man I will boast, but on my own behalf I will not boast, except of my weaknesses. Though if I wish to boast, I shall not be a fool, for I shall be speaking the truth. But I refrain from it, so that no one may think more of me than he sees in me or hears from me (2 Cor. 11:21–12:6).

I appreciate Paul's openness, and the fact that, when Paul has overstated his case, he feels secure enough to admit it as well:

I have been a fool! You forced me to it, for I ought to have been commended by you. For I am not at all inferior to these superlative apostles, even though I am nothing. The signs of a true apostle were performed among you in all patience, with signs and wonders and mighty works (2 Cor. 12:11–12).

Though Paul apologizes to the Corinthians for his overwhelming directness, that apology does not negate the basic healthiness of Paul's approach to the human need for recognition. The unfortunate element within and behind these texts is that the Corinthian Christians did not themselves have enough resources to be able to honor Paul without the prompting.

But what is of vital importance for us is to note that Paul does not confuse admiration with love. The recognition that Paul wanted to receive for his deeds is *not* the belovedness spoke of his life. Recognition is one of the benefits of the rim and hub relationship (we'll talk about this later, too). But the belovedness spoke is something much more generic and fundamental. Our belovedness is the upward spoke of human worth that is founded upon the decision of God. Admiration experiences fluctuate, because that is the nature of recognition and reward. The line of our achievements never slants constantly upward with success upon success; rather, it shudders with shocks and pressures of adversity, and surges with breakthroughs of growth. But the belovedness spoke stays in place through the disapproval from friends and the excitement of praise. The belovedness spoke is what keeps us humble in the times of richness and grateful in the times that are lean.

I am convinced that the greatest cure for pride in a human being is not the humiliation of disapproval, but the free and uncomplicated gift of affirmation. It was because of the basic spoke of belovedness that the apostle Paul was honest enough and secure enough to share autobiographically about the lean moments of his life:

> And to keep me from being too elated by the abundance of revelations, a thorn was given me in the flesh, a messenger of Satan, to harass me, to keep me from being too elated. Three times I besought the Lord about this, that it should leave me; but he said to me, "My grace is sufficient for you, for my power is made perfect in weakness." I will all the more gladly boast of my weaknesses, that the power of

Christ may rest upon me. For the sake of Christ, then, I am content with weaknesses, insults, hardships, persecutions, and calamities; for when I am weak, then I am strong (2 Cor. 12:7-10).

The two spokes of sinfulness and belovedness, taken together, provide the balance. They go together. We are finally able to welcome the knowledge of the sinfulness spoke because that discovery brings us to the hub:

God chose what is low and despised in the world, even things that are not, to bring to nothing things that are, so that no human being might boast in the presence of God. He is the source of your life in Christ Jesus, whom God made our wisdom, our righteousness and sanctification and redemption; therefore, as it is written, "Let him who boasts, boast of the Lord" (1 Cor. 1:23-31).

The belovedness spoke is the discovery of the surprise love of God—the realization that I am loved just as I am—the real me, loved by God. When this realization breaks in upon us in dynamic, antiphonal relationship to the sinfulness realization, a durable and unshakable balance is created within the wheel. The same Jesus Christ who is Lord of truth is Lord of love. He who knows about my life cares about my life.

But as it is true that there is a natural human resistance toward facing up to the sinfulness spoke, ironically, it is also true that there is a natural emotional/intellectual resistance toward the acceptance of the belovedness spoke. We human beings have a very hard time really believing that we are loved, and we have great difficulty trusting and putting our weight down upon the love of God toward us. As there are persons who will not agree with the reality of the sinfulness spoke and will claim for themselves special exemption from all frailty, so also there are people who insist that every spoke in their life is a sinfulness spoke.

They have no confidence in their worthiness and feel totally rejected. They are like Mr. Fearing in *Pilgrim's Progress:*

> [Mr. Honest.] Then it seems he was well at last.
>
> Great-heart. Yes, yes; I never had doubt about him; he was a man of a choice spirit, only he was always kept very low, and that made his life so burdensome to himself, and so troublesome to others. He was above all tender of sin. He was so afraid of doing injuries to others, that he often would deny himself of that which was lawful because he would not offend.
>
> Hon. But what should be the reason that such a good man should be all his days so much in the dark?
>
> Great-heart. There are two sorts of reasons for it. One is, the wise God will have it so; some must pipe and some must weep. Now Mr. Fearing was one that played upon this Base; he and his fellows sound the Sackbut, whose notes are more doleful than the notes of other Music are; though not at all for that profession that begins not in heaviness of mind. The first string that the Musician usually touches is the Base, when he intends to put all in tune. God also plays upon this string first, when he sets the soul in tune for himself. Only here was the imperfection of Mr. Fearing: he could play upon no other Music but this, till towards his latter end.[3]

I remember a conversation I had some time ago with a university student in Berkeley. I had made the comment to him, which was a truthful observation on my part, that I knew he had a great future in his studies and I felt he was a very likable person. He said to me, "If you have a few minutes, Mr. Palmer, I can disprove your opinion." As I listened to him, I realized that he was a young person who was talking too much about himself to himself, and that he needed more information. All of his spokes looked very much alike to him now, and though he did not speak of them in classic theological "sinfulness" terms, that is how he saw them. Wherever he searched into himself, he saw inadequacy, and that is really at the heart of what the New Testament word for "sin" means: "to miss the mark."

I asked him if he would be willing to consider some other inputs, and he said that he was. I suggested that he read the New Testament and C. S. Lewis's *Surprised by Joy*. I wanted him to discover God's view of who he was and is. I knew he was in for a surprise, because when he found out who God is he would also find himself:

> No slightest hint was vouchsafed me that there ever had been or ever would be any connection between God and Joy. If anything, it was the reverse. I had hoped that the heart of reality might be of such a kind that we can best symbolize it as a place; instead, I found it to be a Person. For all I knew, the total rejection of what I called Joy might be one of the demands, might be the very first demand, He would make upon me.[4]

The surprise of the good news is that this very love that enables us to love God and empowers us with the resources to love others also sets us free to love ourselves!

4.

THE UNIQUENESS AND
THE UNITY

There is a second set of spokes in the human wheel, too.
I'll call this second group the unique feelings and yearnings we each bring with us into our relationship with the
center—Jesus Christ. No human being comes to Jesus
empty-handed, just as no climber reaches a summit on
bare feet. We come to the center because the Center has
won us, and this means that we bring with us a totality of
feelings and concerns and quests and equipment.

I am referring to such yearnings as those for happiness,
joy, truth, justice, fellowship, selfhood, peace, identity.
Some of these feelings may be very openly felt and
known, or some may be so deeply etched in the early
formation of our characters that we may not fully understand them for long stretches of time; only later will they
emerge in our self-understanding and consciousness.

These yearnings are, by their essential nature, dynamic
and ever-changing spokes in the wheel. In each human
personality, their mixture and expression differ. One person may have a more fully developed set of fellowship
spoke needs than another. One has an exuberant joy
spoke, while another a contemplative joy spoke. What is
different in each person is the combination of yearnings

and feelings that make up the personality. What is the same in each is the common hub. And the yearnings and feelings themselves are shaped and deepened by contact with the hub and the rim. When we discover the Lordship, the centrality, of Jesus Christ—when he is the hub of our wheel—we find our feelings and yearnings fulfilled in him. He integrates and balances them into the wheel.

Another set of spokes that each human being has I'll call the event spokes. These are the *givens*, the event facts about who we are—race, family, sexual nature, intelligence, health. These are also dynamic spokes; they change in form and intensity throughout our lives. And there are turbulent feelings and yearnings that accompany these event spokes. But what gives these their special character is that we do not have control over their beginnings—only over their ongoing role in our lives. For instance, I do not have the option of choosing my sex, my race, my intelligence, or my family, but I spend my whole life working with feelings and attitudes toward these event spokes of my unique existence. Whether I am short or tall is an event spoke; but all of my life I either accept or reject, embrace or resent that particular spoke. These event spokes, then, deeply affect the yearnings and feelings spokes. They impact the rim and hub and put strains upon the hub and the rim—but that is the way the wheel is intended to work.

The fourth set of spokes are the gifts, the talents, the work that emerge during my lifetime. These are the most changeable of all the spokes. The spiritual gifts about which Paul instructs the Corinthians in 1 Corinthians 12 are part of this set of spokes, as are also the unique talents and work opportunities and tasks that make up our individual lives.

Now let me make two observations about these four sets of spokes. First, when Jesus Christ is the hub, there are more spokes in our lives than with any other hub. This is because Jesus Christ integrates more different kinds of spokes than any other hub is able or willing to integrate.

Let me explain this fact. If the hub of my life were something else—my family for example—I would soon realize that the family is not able to integrate the total spectrum of spokes. This is because, as great as the family is, there are event spokes that will shatter the wheel that has family as its hub. An event spoke such as death is the destructive foe of the family hub; the family as convergent point cannot bear such volcanic upheaval as death. It is asking too much of father and mother and children to integrate such a devastating spoke.

Think of another example. There are people who are so completely caught up in a particular career aspiration that their giftedness or their work becomes the hub of their existence. But that hub is unable to integrate the complexity of spokes that inevitably come into the life of a human being. It cannot resolve the full possibilities of human yearnings nor the full possibilities of time and event.

The Broadway musical play, *A Chorus Line*, gives some helpful insights into the meaning of convergence. Each of the young dancers is trying out for a limited number of places in the chorus line of a show. The unseen director speaks from the darkness of the theater to each young performer, and as the play proceeds, the lives of these dancers are explored. One of the most powerful and dramatic scenes in the show is that moment in which the director asks a young performer what he plans for his life if he is unable to dance. The question is brutal because it allows an unacceptable spoke into the wheel which has Broadway as its hub. In that instant, as in others throughout the play, the dramatic focus is not upon the tryout line for a future show but the tryout line for life itself. An art form, a profession, or a talent is a merciless and false hub that will finally destroy the very wheel that has chosen it as its true center—"Who am I anyway? Am I my résumé?" There are many men and women who have had human relationship and justice spokes, and self-respect spokes disconnected by the insatiable demands of the career hub.

The story can be repeated over and over again with countless false hubs. What of the church as a hub? Will it serve any better? It, too, is inadequate as the hub. The Christian church as the center of our lives can be just as dehumanizing as any other false center, because the church was never intended by God to be the center of our lives. To ask that a Christian fellowship be in and of itself the convergent point places too much weight upon the church.

Only Jesus Christ as hub has the authority to integrate the many complex parts, the many spokes, that make up our life into a meaningful whole. He is able to forgive sin. Therefore, human sinfulness does not crack the wheel when brought to the hub. Christ is able to fulfill the total range of human aspiration. Therefore, every human quest and ambition finds its deepest resonance and fulfillment in the one who is the Source of all human yearnings. There is no giftedness that we may develop or discover that threatens Jesus Christ as center. One mark of a person who has found Christ as center is that the richness that comes from the many ingredients of life is encouraged, not squelched.

One of the features of a false hub is that it promotes an artificial simplification of the wheel and its spokes. A certain few approved spokes are encouraged, and others are discouraged. For instance a very highly developed obedience spoke may be encouraged, and a heavy zealousness spoke may be approved, but the marvelous mixture of unique freedom spokes may be absent, because the false hub is threatened by them. This is one reason that people caught up in movements or causes which have become the all-encompassing center for them are often capable of impressive sacrifice and almost total commitment of time.

The reason for this is not the richness of their center but its inadequacy. They have been permitted so very few spokes by their new center that they have little else to do but redouble their efforts.

But for the man or woman who discovers Jesus Christ as hub, there are many spokes. They are not only permitted but encouraged. This does not mean they are undisciplined and chaotic. There is a discipline of balance in the wheel; an ambition spoke is disciplined by a companion justice spoke, just as the sinfulness spoke is balanced by the belovedness spoke. A love-for-family spoke thrives in dynamic tension with the love-for-neighbor spoke.

Such is the wheel that has Christ as its center. Listen to Paul as he celebrates the richness of the spokes:

> Now there are varieties of gifts, but the same Spirit; and there are varieties of service, but the same Lord; and there are varieties of working, but it is the same God who inspires them all in every one. To each is given the manifestation of the Spirit for the common good. To one is given through the Spirit the utterance of wisdom, and to another the utterance of knowledge according to the same Spirit, to another faith by the same Spirit, to another gifts of healing by the one Spirit, to another the working of miracles, to another prophecy, to another the ability to distinguish between spirits, to another various kinds of tongues, to another the interpretation of tongues. All these are inspired by one and the same Spirit, who apportions to each one individually as he wills. For just as the body is one and has many members, and all the members of the body, though many, are one body, so it is with Christ. For by one Spirit we were all baptized into one body—Jews or Greeks, slaves or free—and all were made to drink of one Spirit. For the body does not consist of one member but of many (1 Cor. 12:4–14).

The second observation that I want to make is this: the spokes do better as spokes than as false hubs. The company I work for is best served by an employee who has a healthy balance in his or her life, and who sees work as an important part, but not the center, of the whole. My family thrives when I see it as part of a good and larger context which includes within its own design a meaningful love for the family that grows out of my love for God and his love for me. This is better, then, for the family than if the family were the center of my being. Jesus Christ enriches our relationships, and enables me to be a better father (or a better mother, a better husband, a better wife, a better son, a better daughter) than I would be if my life were totally submerged and centered upon my family relationships.

The same is true of the church, the gifts and work of the Christian, social concerns, and political movements. Each of these is better fulfilled when they themselves are not worshiped and obeyed as if they were the center. Only Jesus Christ deserves to be the center; when he is that true center, he then "elicits significance from all sorts of details in the whole work which we had hitherto neglected."[1]

Paul opens his Corinthian letter with this concern as his major theme:

> So let no one boast of men. For all things are yours, whether Paul or Apollos or Cephas or the world or life or death or the present or the future, all are yours; and you are Christ's; and Christ is God's (1 Cor. 3:21–23).

And this centering of life upon the true center is the theme throughout the whole New Testament, not just the letters of Paul. Jesus himself taught the disciples this truth by means of the parable of the door in John 10; he makes the promise in that parable that all of the other themes and events of our lives are fulfilled, not when they seek to be that door themselves, but when they enter *through* the door:

I am the door; if any one enters by me, he will be saved, and will go in and out and find pasture. The thief comes only to steal and kill and destroy; I came that they may have life, and have it abundantly (John 19:9–10).

5.

THE RIM HAS
TWO PARTS

So far in this book I have attempted to present a contemporary study of Paul's discipleship teaching in 1 and 2 Corinthians using the image of the wheel as a modern parable. We have already looked at the hub of the wheel, the convergence point of all existence—Jesus Christ. This was Paul's principle theological concern in the two Corinthian letters. Wherever you turn in Corinthians, whatever particular subject may be under discussion, it soon becomes clear that all themes point to the centrality of Jesus Christ.

In Paul's theology, every discipleship question is really a question about the implications of the forgiveness we have in Christ. Every ethical issue is illuminated by the meaning for life that God has already revealed in the incarnation of Jesus Christ. The question of the mission of the Christian and the motivation for that mission is for Paul a question about the meaning of the authority and the love of Christ. In short, Paul is a centralist in these two books, and there is no way to make any sense of the advice, either ethical or ecclesiastical, either evangelical or personal, apart from his decisive convergence-point theological persuasion.

In my view, Paul's centralism is the correct stance for all

discipleship and theological questions. I think Karl Barth
has expressed the ethical implications of this centralism in
a very fresh way in this commentary on the sentence in the
Apostles' Creed, "I believe in the forgiveness of sins":

> And now we must not say that it is not enough to live by
> forgiveness "alone." This objection has been raised against
> the Creed and strengthened against the Reformers. What
> folly! As though just this, the forgiveness of sins, were not
> the only thing by which we live, the power of all powers! As
> though everything were not said in that phrase! It is pre-
> cisely when we are aware that "God is for me," that we are
> in the true sense *responsible*. For from that standpoint and
> from that alone is there a real ethic, have we a criterion of
> good and evil. So living by forgiveness is never by any
> means passivity, but Christian living in full activity.
> Whether we prefer to describe it as great freedom or as strict
> discipline, as piety or as true worldliness, as private
> morality or as social morality, whether we regard this life
> under the sign of the great hope or under the sign of daily
> patience, in any case we live solely by forgiveness.[1]

If the hub is Paul's primary focus in the two Corinthian
letters, then his next concern has to do with the spokes. I
mean by that the particular discipleship questions and
lifestyle questions the Corinthian Christians were facing
day by day—their specific sinfulness spokes and belovedness spokes and feeling, event, and giftedness spokes.
Paul devotes a significant amount of space in these letters
to the whole subject of the meaning of personal existence.
He speaks about the meaning of sexuality and marriage
and includes personal advice on those questions (see 1
Cor. 6 and 7). He writes in detail about personal suffering
(see 2 Cor. 1 and 5); he writes about personal freedom and
ethical responsibility (see 1 Cor. 8, 9, 10). He counsels
those at Corinth who are slaves (1 Cor. 7:17–24), and he

counsels his readers about personal generosity as a mark of discipleship (2 Cor. 9).

There is one other principle focus of the Corinthian letters that has to do with the wheel parable, and that focus is the rim of the wheel. This third concern of Paul will be the subject of this chapter.

The rim of a bicycle has two parts. First, it has an aluminum alloy inner circle which ties in the spokes and completes their relationship to the hub and to each other; this rim unites the spokes at the circumference of the wheel, just as the hub unites them at the center. The second part of the rim is its outer circle—the pneumatic tire through which the wheel meets the road. The rim is the weakest part of the wheel; unlike the fine steel of the hub, its metal is softer and lighter. Surprisingly, the tire is the weakest part of all. But it all works, and it works very well, as weight, movement, and energy are united in the wheel assembly. Because of the flexible strength of the wheel, its spokes and rim assembly can take terrific and sudden shocks. Even with the loss of one or two spokes, the wheel is able to carry weight and transfer the forward-thrust pedaling force of the biker. All of this is possible because of the engineering design of the rim-spoke-hub relationship. It is designed to spread out the stress and equalize the load.

The rim in my understanding of this modern parable is the *koinonia* (the fellowship) experiences into which we are drawn. The family into which we were born is such a rim; the family we establish by marriage is another. The Christian church is also such a rim, and it is this extended family and faith with which Paul is especially concerned in the Corinthian letters.

Now we want to examine that rim, and what Paul has said about it in 1 and 2 Corinthians. At the very opening of his letter to the Corinthians, Paul described the rim with great affection and respect: "I give thanks to God always for you" (1 Cor. 1:4). And he took a great deal of care explaining the process by which the rim comes into being and operates with relation to the spokes and the hub. The role of the Holy Spirit is especially important in this process. It is the Holy Spirit who binds the believers to Christ and who also binds the believers to each other.

The ministry of the Holy Spirit as unfolded in the Bible has always been twofold. His first function has been to assure men and women of the Center. John Calvin said, "The whole of it comes to this, the Holy Spirit is the bond by which Christ binds us to himself." Paul expresses this first ministry of the Holy Spirit with great forcefulness in 1 Corinthians 12:2–3:

> You know that when you were heathen, you were led astray to dumb idols, however you may have been moved. Therefore I want you to understand that no one speaking by the Spirit of God ever says "Jesus be cursed!" and no one can say "Jesus is Lord" except by the Holy Spirit.

Paul's point is very clear. We are assured of the Lordship of Jesus Christ because in the mystery of the Holy Spirit we have been personally convinced—so that we are able to say, "Jesus Christ is my Lord."

The second ministry of the Holy Spirit is to be the creator of the church. The Holy Spirit who binds us to Christ also binds us to each other. In both cases our uniqueness and freedom have not been destroyed by the ministry of assurance, and that is the mystery Paul tells us of in 2 Corinthians 3:16–18:

> When a man turns to the Lord the veil is removed. Now the Lord is the Spirit, and where the Spirit of the Lord is, there is freedom. And we all, with unveiled face, beholding the

glory of the Lord, are being changed into his likeness from one degree of glory to another; for this comes from the Lord who is the Spirit.

We are bound and set free at the same moment! Just as a scientist who discovers the truth in an experiment is bound to the truth now discovered, the researcher is also set free from the false pathways and failed experiments of error. The successful adventurer is set free to now pursue the breakthroughs of the truth now discovered. Paul expresses the second ministry of the Holy Spirit as follows.

> For just as the body is one and has many members, and all the members of the body, though many, are one body, so it is with Christ. For by one Spirit we were all baptized into one body—Jews or Greeks, slaves or free—and all were made. to drink of one Spirit (1 Cor. 12:12–13).

We who live twenty centuries later than Paul and the Corinthians are intended by God to experience the same twofold ministry of the Holy Spirit today as much as it was the experience of first-century Christians. Our freedom is not swept away by the assurance ministry of the Holy Spirit, and therefore we must make many decisions of our own at each step of the assurance process. This is why it takes time to become a believer in Christ, and it takes time to become a part of the rim. A journey on our part is involved in both experiences of assurance. This dynamic nature of the assurance experience is the reason Paul wrote letters to the early Christians; this is the reason he asked them to think through the meaning of faith, hope, love, and all other Christian themes. Faith is usually not a single moment of overwhelming discovery. It takes time to grow a friendship with Jesus Christ as Lord and Savior; it also takes time to grow a friendship with the forever family that comes into existence by faith. Let us probe the dynamic process of becoming a living part of the rim—the body of Christ.

What do you think of the rim because of your own experience with it? Do you have mixed feelings? Would your description be like two descriptions of Paul's? He referred to the church as "... those sanctified in Christ Jesus, called to be saints together with all those who in every place call on the name of our Lord Jesus Christ, both their Lord and ours" (1 Cor. 1:2), but just a few verses later he said, "It has been reported to me by Chloe's people that there is quarreling among you, my brethren" (1 Cor. 1:11). It is my experience that most people—certainly I can speak for myself—have mixed feelings about the rim. On the one side there is the joyous experience of fellowship and the profound respect for so great a company: "We are the body of Christ." But on the other side, it is sometimes difficult to really feel at home in the Christian church.

Why the respectful joy on the one side and on the other this uneasiness? The uneasiness many people feel toward the Christian church may originate from one of two opposite reasons, and in some cases from a combination of both. In the first place, it may originate in a general feeling of inferiority toward the Christian rim, its task in history, and its distinguished worldwide fellowship. When I consider my own nature, then this feeling of inadequacy comes to the surface; I become unsure and hesitant about my own worthiness to be considered a part of so great a rim. I seem so unlike the other Christians and so much less impressive; therefore rather than face the possibility of future rejection I withdraw from possibility of fellowship before it can happen.

Paul was aware that this very hesitancy was a reality in the situation at Corinth. He replied to this feeling by using the analogy of the body:

If the foot should say, "Because I am not a hand, I do not belong to the body," that would not make it any less a part of the body. And if the ear should say, "Because I am not an eye, I do not belong to the body," that would not make it any less a part of the body. If the whole body were an eye, where would be the hearing? If the whole body were an ear, where would be the sense of smell? But as it is, God arranged the organs in the body, each one of them, as he chose. (1 Cor. 12:15–18).

Paul's argument was that we human beings by ourselves and unto ourselves do not understand such large questions as who we really are and what our true importance to the whole is. Paul makes the point that it takes the larger relationship to really answer such questions. How can a hand of itself possibly be expected to understand its potential importance until it is introduced to the rest of the body?

But Paul makes an even more important point. He maintains that, even though we may feel totally inadequate, that self-depreciative feeling does not change the fundamental fact of our belovedness spoke and of our giftedness spokes. The feeling of inadequacy or inward feelings of unacceptability do not negate the decision God has made about us and our worth. We are a part of the Body of Christ primarily because of *Christ's* decision.

This decision does not mean that my freedom was set aside by God's grace, so that I am forced to become a disciple of Jesus Christ. Paul insisted on the freedom of the Christian throughout his Corinthian letters; indeed, that is the point of the letters. He was challenging the Corinthians to make their very own real decisions in response to God's love. But it is God's decision to love us, and his decision to give us unique gifts so that we are very important to the people around us, just as the hand is essential to the eye in protecting it from danger, or after a dust

storm. This is a prior decision on God's part. Our negative
feelings about ourselves do not cancel out that real importance, though it is true that our negative feelings hold us
back and are harmful to us and to the people around us.

For example, the importance that a father has in the life
and development of his son or daughter is not erased just
because the father feels he is a failure and therefore in one
way or another walks away from the family. It just means
he is not around when he is needed. He may make the
choice to avoid the people who need him, but his choice
does not mean that they no longer need him or that he has
no unique or irreplaceable gifts. As the hand is needed by
the body, so he is needed by his family. The question is
whether he is there or not.

The second reason for uneasiness about the church
stems from an equally disastrous self-misunderstanding—
that is, the feeling of superiority toward the rim. Paul
makes use of his anatomical analogy to address this feeling
also:

> The eye cannot say to the hand, "I have no need of you,"
> nor again the head to the feet, "I have no need of you." On
> the contrary, the parts of the body which seem to be weaker
> are indispensable, and those parts of the body which we
> think less honorable we invest with the greater honor, and
> our unpresentable parts are treated with greater modesty,
> which our more presentable parts do not require. But God
> has so composed the body, giving the greater honor to the
> inferior part, that there may be no discord in the body, but
> that the members may have the same care for one another.
> If one member suffers, all suffer together; if one member is
> honored, all rejoice together. Now you are the body of
> Christ and individually members of it (1 Cor. 12:21–27).

It is not hard to uncover well-validated stories about the
failures of the Christian church. If we find enough of these
stories we may individually come to the conclusion that it

would be better and even perhaps more honest to go it alone rather than to be slowed down by a sense of obligation to such an ineffective fellowship. The accusation of mediocrity, of embarrassing weakness in the church, becomes the argument of the "eye," which foolishly dismisses the "hand" with the salvo, "I have no need of you!"

This bold assertion of self-confidence and independence not only is false; when carried to its full course, it becomes idolatrous. No human being was meant to exist alone, any more than the spokes of a wheel can exist alone or parts of the body exist alone. Spokes need both the hub at the center and the rim at the circumference. The eye does need the hand, and this need is not its shame but a part of its glory—the glory of the eye is seen in its balanced and appropriate contrast to the rest of the body. It is the uniqueness of both the eye and the hand that gives to each its wonder and beauty. Without the relationship between the parts, the glory would be lost in excessive repetition. A severed hand is horrible, not beautiful. But, united to a whole body, the hand is an artistic triumph.

We must never sell short the Christian church. Once a person has experienced the joy of Christian fellowship, the hesitancy that comes either from feelings of inferiority or of superiority is resolved. This is because of an important fact that must not be overlooked: the rim works! The rim is God's way to bring an individual's spokes together, to enable individual Christians to discover their own fulfillment. The principle involved in this is both psychologically and spiritually true. What the parable of a bicycle wheel (and also the parable of the body) is teaching is that we need fellowship with Jesus Christ—the hub—and with others—the rim—in order to fully discover and fulfill even our own potential. It is simply the way we have been made to work. This is not bad news to hold us back, but good news to set us free. It does not slow us down, but in fact enables us to reach our greatest speed and our full stride. This is the joyous side of being a part of the Christian fellowship that is called the church.

We can make two interesting observations at this point about *how* the rim works. The rim of a bicycle wheel works first of all because it is flexibly strong. Its strength is not the rigid strength of an iron and oak wagon wheel, but a flexible strength that can absorb more speed and road shock than is necessary for the covered-wagon wheel. The flexible pneumatic tire of a 747 wheel allows it to withstand the sudden force of the landing jet—force that would shatter a rigid covered-wagon wheel. Still another example of rigid strength would be the solid stone construction of the pyramids or of the Washington monument. It is the sheer downward weight of the stones that gives those structures their strength. But where there are earthquakes, high winds, and sudden jolts, then a different kind of strength is needed, and that is flexible strength—as in the suspension structure of the Golden Gate Bridge.

Spiritually, the flexible strength of the Christian church is the reality of the gospel that keeps the church resilient. The gospel sustains the church—forgives, heals, mends. Where broken relationships occur in the fellowship of the church, it is only that gospel of the true, living Center—Jesus Christ—that can reunite the church. Therefore, the need of the church when stresses overtake it is not so much an infusion of more rigid authority, but of more healing from the gospel.

This brings us to the second point about how the rim works: the secret of its power and its proper functioning is the *hub*. The relationship with the hub is the secret to the roundness of the rim, and also is the source of its flexible strength. So when the rim faces pressures and road stress, what it needs is not to become more rigid in itself, but to develop a more obedient connection to the hub.

Of course, there are times when the rim needs repair

work. Punctures in the tire must be sealed; loosened spokes must be retightened. As I see it, this is the role of reform and renewal movements in the Christian fellowship. They are raised up by God to rebalance, strengthen, and repair the rim—first in its relationship to the hub, then in its relationship to its fellowship, and also in relationship to the road (the world). Renewal movements face up to the inadequacies of the rim. Because there are usually inadequacies in the church's fellowship or worship or ethical response to the gospel of Jesus Christ and to the world, there are times when it needs to be decisively challenged and renewed—rebalanced.

It is very interesting to especially note the practical questions and concerns that the apostle Paul had on his mind when he counseled the church in 1 and 2 Corinthians. As we have mentioned, he was concerned most of all about the true center of the church. But there were other themes on his heart as well. He was concerned about specific attitudes of the church, and in this regard he scolded the Corinthian Christians for their pride and isolation. Paul squarely rebuked the church at Corinth over several concrete issues: open immorality in the church, the lack of discipline in their fellowship (1 Cor. 5, 6), the lavish style of their life (1 Cor. 4), the improper observance of the sacrament of the Lord's Supper (1 Cor. 11), confusion in the church about mystical gifts (1 Cor. 14). Paul also positively taught the doctrine of gifts for the church and of the holy restraint of love upon those gifts (1 Cor. 13). He corrected misconceptions about the future hope (1 Cor. 15). Paul urged the church to show pastoral sensitivity within the fellowship (2 Cor. 2), and to face up to its mission in the world (2 Cor. 5). He urged openness (2 Cor. 6, 7), and generosity toward the suffering Christians in Jerusalem (2 Cor. 9). Finally, he urged the church not to close itself off from Christians in other places (2 Cor. 10, 11).

Throughout his two letters, the apostle sought by his

advice and by the example of his own life to balance the rim and to keep it flexible, strong, and useful. I realize, when I think back over the years of my own personal journey, that at every important crossroad of my life there were Christians who, like Paul with the Corinthians, walked alongside me in my life. Their stories were parallel to my own story; my life has not been formed apart from them. I have needed the brothers and sisters of the Christian church to enable me in my own life. And I always say to members of our fellowship at Berkeley, when they leave our city to move on to the next part of their journey, "Find the Christians." Find the rim.

Make no mistake about it, the rim is not the hub, and it never will be. The Christian fellowship is therefore never an absolute reference point in itself. The hub is the only absolute, and the church has authority only as it faithfully points to the hub. The only authority that we in the church possess is derived from our faithfulness to the law and the gospel. When the church is disobedient to the truth of the gospel, then the renewal-reform prophets are needed to rebalance the rim. But we belong to the rim, even though we are fully aware of its dents and its continuous need for reform and renewal. We rejoice in the rim because of the life of the gospel of Jesus Christ at work in it. We rejoice in the rim because of the exciting benefits we receive from it. Some Christians and some congregations of Christians have learned how rich the benefits of the rim can be. I know Christians who have learned how to encourage, and I know from experience how much that means. I'll never forget an incident that happened at a retirement reception that our church was having for George and Vera Kerr. George had been our chief custodian for some twenty-five years. During the presentation at the reception, I asked George and Vera if they would share any thoughts with the crowd of well-wishers. Vera turned to me and said how well she remembered when I was an undergraduate at the University of California at Berkeley and the two summers during my seminary training when I worked in the Berkeley church with the youth. She told me that during that summer of 1954 she decided to pray regularly for me and for my ministry. She said, "You know, Earl, I have prayed for you ever since—when you were in Seattle, in Manila, and now back here in Berkeley where you first started." This is the beloved rim. (Thank you, Vera!)

6.

AMBASSADORS

In the preceding chapter we said that the rim of a bicycle wheel has two parts—the metal inner circle and the outer circle, the tire, which actually makes contact with the road. In this chapter, I want to look at this outer circle in the light of the wheel parable.

If we look at the rim of the wheel as representing for the Christian the body of fellow believers—the church—then the outer circle, the part which brings the whole of the wheel and the world together, stands for the relationship Christians have with the world we live in, and the task we have in the world. In Paul's letter to the Corinthians, he calls this task our *ambassadorship* to the world:

> For the love of Christ controls us, because we are convinced that one has died for all; therefore all have died. And he died for all, that those who live might live no longer for themselves but for him who for their sake died and was raised. From now on, therefore, we regard no one from a human point of view, even though we once regarded Christ from a human point of view, we regard him thus no longer. Therefore, if any one is in Christ, he is a new creation; the old has passed away, behold, the new has come. All this is from God, who through Christ reconciled us to himself and

gave us the ministry of reconciliation; that is, in Christ God was reconciling the world to himself, not counting their trespasses against them, and entrusting to us the message of reconciliation. So we are ambassadors for Christ, God making his appeal through us. We beseech you on behalf of Christ, be reconciled to God. For our sake he made him to be sin who knew no sin, so that in him we might become the righteousness of God (2 Cor. 5:14-21).

A close reading of this text gives some important clues to the meaning of that ambassadorship. We relate to the world in terms of a great *given,* and that given is God's decision about the world. In other words, because of Jesus Christ we have a very special perspective toward the world, a new way of looking at it. It is not new as far as God is concerned; God has always loved the world he created, and there are many signs of this prior love throughout the Old Testament—in the Law and the Psalms and the Prophets. But in Jesus Christ, the love of God for the world has been fulfilled and made victorious. We who know Jesus Christ as Savior and Lord have entered into the discovery of that ancient mystery.

This is Paul's main point in 2 Corinthians 5. According to Paul, the victory of Christ's love over death is the new creation, and he tells the Corinthians that we are to understand the whole created order in the light of that victory. Therefore, the old hatreds, the old vicious cycles of anger and fear between neighbors are not the last word; rather, it is the powerful act of Christ's love that has the final say. We are to be ambassadors of this good news and of its healing implications to our generation.

Paul calls this ambassadorship the ministry of reconciliation. This is by no means an uncomplicated task—as anyone who ever tried to mediate a labor-management dispute, a racial mistrust, or a conflict in the family knows. Nevertheless, the task of the Christian fellowship is to be just that kind of healing presence in the real world, where the gravest of all human and social needs is the need for reconciliation and the justice that goes with all genuine reconciliation.

With such an important task, we can see the vital importance of the holy colony of the church as the rim of the wheel. We who make up the rim will need all of the skills and gifts each unique Christian has to offer working together in order to fulfill this mandate. In addition, as Paul also makes clear in the letter to the Corinthians, the complicated crises that the church finds in the world are the same crises we find within the church itself. Christians need the forgiveness and powerful love of Christ within the inner rim, as much as the world needs this love in the outer rim.

A fact that complicates our mission in the world is that, though the world and the church *need* the justice-reconciliation of Christ's love, the world and the church rarely *want* that justice-reconciliation. There are many other things most of us *think* we need more than forgiveness—such as spiritual or physical power, special advantages, and a thousand variations of the desire to control. Therefore, Paul wisely uses the term "ambassador" to remind the Christians that the ministry of reconciliation requires skill and wisdom.

I have a friend, Tim Buscheck, who is an expert high-speed biker, and he has helped me understand an interesting fact about biking. At very high speeds, one of the very greatest dangers in biking occurs when the tire slips off the rim; the rider is then left with a bare metal rim on the pavement. It takes very skillful riding to keep this from happening. The bike needs its tire! The church (the rim) also needs its mission relationship with the world (the tire), but it requires the skill of ambassadorship and statesmanship to keep that relationship fully connected and engaged.

Injustice is rarely a simple, straightforward opposition

to be faced, because injustice always dresses itself up with the rhetoric of peace or progress or success. It will be the task of the rim to stay in as close as possible to the world and to skillfully present the claims of the true reconciliation of God's love and truth into a setting that is often hostile and closed tight by self-deception.

If it were not for the authenticating power of the Holy Spirit at work in the gospel itself, there would be little possibility of the kind of substantial breakthroughs that are needed for healing to happen. But, in fact, the authority of God himself has spoken by word and by work, and Jesus Christ is that eternal speech of God. He has identified fully with us, even in facing the death we all face. Therefore, his death in our behalf has the power to profoundly reconcile every possible human estrangement. The reconciliation we human beings need in order to become whole and to set right the confusion of our self-centered lives is the reconciliation that must come from the one who made us in the first place. Paul calls the task of bringing this reconciliation a ministry, because it is God's will to make use of his people in the world in a concrete way.

It is very important to keep clear the distinction between what we as ambassadors are given to do and what we are not given to do. We bring the message of redemption, but we are not the Redeemer. Paul clearly preserves that holy restraint upon us as the servants of God. Jesus Christ, and he alone, is the Redeemer. He is the one who has died and conquered death. This restraint preserves the rim from mistaken and cultic or messianic notions about itself. As we have already emphasized, the rim is to be the rim; the hub must be the hub.

What then is the ministry of reconciliation in the world? It is the ministry of "alongsideness." It means that the Christian disciple as an individual and as a part of the larger fellowship of Christians is called by Christ to be in the world as a concrete presence of truth and love and life.

This can be a costly presence, because the Christian is called to *be* as much as to *speak*. We are to be in the world with the life of Christ in us (2 Cor. 5:15), and we are to share the truth of the gospel (2 Cor. 5:20).

Earlier in 2 Corinthians, Paul portrayed the spiritual source and strategy for this ministry in his great paragraph about the word *paracaletos*, a word that is used for the Holy Spirit in John's Gospel and which means, literally, "to come alongside." The Revised Standard Version translates each use of this word with the English word *comfort*, which in my view is hardly an adequate word to express the full force of the play upon the idea "to come alongside." Notice the following text, and in your own reading substitute the phrase, "to come alongside" in each place where the RSV has placed the word *comfort*:

> Blessed be the God and Father of our Lord Jesus Christ, the Father of mercies and God of all comfort, who comforts us in all our affliction, so that we may be able to comfort those who are in any affliction, with the comfort with which we ourselves are comforted by God. For as we share abundantly in Christ's sufferings, so through Christ we share abundantly in comfort too. If we are afflicted, it is for your comfort and salvation; and if we are comforted, it is for your comfort, which you experience when you patiently endure the same sufferings that we suffer. Our hope for you is unshaken; for we know that as you share in our sufferings, you will also share in our comfort (1:3-7).

Note that we are to express to the world around us that same companionship which we have received from Jesus Christ through the Holy Spirit. As we ourselves have experienced the coming alongside of Christ, so we as ambassadors of Christ are to come alongside the people who hurt in the world—people Jesus Christ died for.

This is our holy task, and the Good News for that task is that Jesus Christ himself authenticates and empowers the church and its message of hope. Jesus Christ changes life, so that if anyone is in Christ he or she is a new creation. This is the power that confirms our ambassadorship to the world.

I remember a recent conversation I had with a man about my own age who had attended the University of California at Berkeley. He had received his degree in fine arts, and as he told me his own story he put it this way: "I was captured by some false dreams and relationships." He told me of twenty years that he spent in the pursuit of these dreams that had now fallen apart in his hands. His dreams had been infiltrated by drugs and ethical shortcuts. Now, in his forties, he was painfully discouraged by broken relationships and the overwhelming feeling of twenty years wasted.

As we talked together, I asked this man if he was willing to consider the radical claims and promises of the Jesus Christ of the New Testament. He said he was and that was why he had decided to ask my advice as a pastor. A sentence came to me, and I said, "You know, Jesus Christ is the great healer, and he is able to heal your life, too." We went on to talk about how Christ integrates and makes our lives whole.

Later on, this man shared with me that the jolt which had helped him to take a new look at everything was the realization that Jesus Christ could actually heal people and make them whole. This means that, regardless of how terribly complicated the situation might be, that situation is not the last word; the Good News is that there is another and a better word. Jesus Christ makes everything new, and that fact is the basis for both the evangelistic and the social justice mandates of the Christian church in the world.

I have personally observed that what gives real power to the Christian witness in the world is the confidence that there is no estrangement, no fear, no violence that cannot

be healed by the tough love of Jesus Christ. It is this confidence in the power of the gospel that gives a Christian the
courage to get in close to human need. It is this confidence
that wins out against escapism, too. Why run away from
life if reconciliation is really possible? It is this confidence
that also motivates the sense of strategy and patience so
that we take the long view rather than panic at each im-
mediate crisis. Healing takes time, but when we live from
hope, we are willing to take the time it takes.

7.

THE BALANCED LIFE

There are three fundamental quests every human being makes. One is the search for *life* itself. This quest takes on many forms and is expressed in many different ways across a broad spectrum of intensity and coloration. It stretches from the most primary struggle to survive, and across the range of colors toward the intricate shades of fulfillment and success—all the distance from basic existence to the fulfillment of the good life. The quest for life is universal, though individual expectations about life are separate and special. One person's lean is another person's fat; one person's blue is another person's gray

Another fundamental quest of all human beings is the quest for *truth*. The Greeks called this quest the search for *logos*, that is, for the meaning of life—its purpose and its goal. For the Jews this was the quest for wisdom, for light that shines upon the pathway: "[Make] your ear attentive to wisdom and [incline] your heart to understanding; for if you cry out for insight and raise your voice for understanding, ... then you will understand the fear of the Lord and find the knowledge of God" (Prov. 2:2-5). In our generation, the truth quest has been primarily seen as the search for personal identity.

A third fundamental quest of all human beings is the search for *love*. This universal quest, like those for truth and life, also stretches across a broad spectrum that includes within it the human desire for companionship, for human friendship, and for the love of God. This profound yearning includes both the need to be loved and the need to give love.

Taken together, these three quests are the marks of what it means to be a human being. And it is the positive fulfillment of these three quests that equals the individual who has reached full potential—the happy woman or man.

At the very opening of the letters to the Corinthians, Paul makes the claim that these fundamental quests converge like profound spokes into the true hub:

> He is the source of your life in Christ Jesus, whom God made our wisdom, our righteousness and sanctification and redemption; therefore, as it is written, "Let him who boasts, boast of the Lord" (1 Cor. 1:30-31).

Note that in these verses Paul affirms that Jesus Christ is our life. He is the source of our truth, and in Christ we discover our growing positive relationship of love. Throughout the two letters to the Corinthians, Paul seeks to grapple with the many variations and expressions of these basic human quests. Paul warns the Corinthians about the false attempts to fulfill these yearnings, and he also teaches in a positive fashion about their genuine fulfillment.

What makes human sinfulness tragic in the most classic sense of that word is the fact that most human sins are made up of good yearnings gone bad. Most of the brutal acts we commit against other human beings and the created order around us are mixed in with these very yearnings for love, truth, and life, but in these cases the yearnings become distorted and off-center. The love of tribe and nation and race may become an absolutely devastating "virtue" when it is distorted into the narrow supernationalism and racism we have known so well in our own century. The yearning for the good life may deteriorate into selfishness and the deadly sin of *luxuria*. The most famous chapter in all of Paul's letters begins with a paragraph that dares to catalogue how virtues like courage, the desire for truth, and mystical knowledge may become totally empty when they are not bound to the good center that is God's love:

> If I speak in the tongues of men and of angels, but have not love, I am a noisy gong or a clanging cymbal. And if I have prophetic powers, and understand all mysteries and all knowledge, and if I have all faith, so as to remove mountains, but have not love, I am nothing. If I give away all I have, and if I deliver my body to be burned, but have not love, I gain nothing (1 Cor. 13:1-3).

It may well have been that it was these three human yearnings that led to the combative breakup of the church at Corinth. The Corinthian Christians divided up, they fractured the rim of the wheel, so that they began to steer separate courses toward the inevitable pathway of privatism and cultism. Perhaps it was the search for truth, trailing off into a smug party spirit, that caused this. Or perhaps it was the search for warm interpersonal relationships—for love—that really motivated the breaking apart of the rim at Corinth. This may sound strange, but the fact is that most of the hurtful exclusiveness which characterizes factionalism is usually created in the beginning so that people may be able to have fellowship with other people they love and want to be near. In such cases it is the quest for love that tumbles in upon itself and becomes cliquish and self-serving.

Think of a third possibility to explain the split at Corinth. Could it be the yearning for life, for fulfillment and self-actualization, that went eccentric and totally confused the meaning of spiritual gifts in the church? We know from reading between the lines in the Corinthian letters that a fascination with spiritual breakthroughs and giftedness had swept through the church at Corinth. The people were very sure of themselves for the wrong reasons: "Already you are filled! Already you have become rich! Without us you have become kings" (1 Cor. 4:8). The feeling of power and success had produced among many people at Corinth the desire for continuous reenforcement of that feeling—and the best way to experience such continual reenforcement is to design a fellowship that has this narrow goal as its chief task. This faction, therefore, was determined not to allow the very "elementary" gospel doctrines of Paul to slow down their development. And they were on their way toward the destruction of the rim at Corinth.

Again, the tragedy of such adriftness is that it begins with yearnings that are normal and healthy. Every quest for virtue needs to remember its true center, or it will do harm. The fact is, the sins of virtue are even more dangerous than what we think of as the gross sins, because they are more easily sheltered from light. For example, I know a person who is honest and totally open in interpersonal relationships. But this "virtue" has become a cover for him which disguises a tendency to be brutal and hurtful in those very relationships. His virtue has become isolated from the Living Center who is the author of honesty. Virtue can become a demon when it is broken away from the context that gives meaning. It is like a spoke or rim trying to be the hub.

Paul sounded the alarm about this to the Corinthians, and the alarm was needed. But what is very impressive to me is that Paul devoted more time to the portrayal of the

positive fulfillment of these deep yearnings than to warn-
ings about their distortion. He was more concerned with
teaching about and modeling in his own life the positive
and winning value of a life that is on center—thriving,
growing, and being all it was meant to be. The two books
of Corinthians are first and foremost books about the balanced Christian life, and only secondarily books about our
problems and imbalances. At this point, then, I want to
examine some of the marks of the balanced life.

For our lives to stay healthy and balanced, we each
need the fulfillment of the three great human quests for
truth, love, and life—by fulfillment I mean daily growth in
these basic resources and values. For this to happen, we
human beings must first of all have a healthy upward
relationship with God. This is our connection with the hub
of the wheel:

> I give thanks to God always for you because of the grace of
> God which was given you in Christ Jesus, that in every way
> you were enriched in him with all speech and all
> knowledge—even as the testimony to Christ was confirmed
> among you—so that you are not lacking in any spiritual gift,
> as you wait for the revealing of our Lord Jesus Christ; who
> will sustain you to the end, guiltless in the day of our Lord
> Jesus Christ. God is faithful, by whom you were called into
> the fellowship of his Son, Jesus Christ our Lord (1 Cor.
> 1:4-9).

This healthy relationship with God is not an art form or
skill as much as it is a daily relationship and walk. And
just as love in the Bible is not an ideal we are to seek,
but a relationship we are invited to experience, so also
are the values of truth and life. I am talking here about
the daily journey of the ordinary Christian in Christian
discipleship—with all the ups and downs that go with that
discipleship. I am talking about prayer, worship, Bible
study, ethical obedience on a step-by-step basis. Apart

from these daily discipleship events, there is no way to keep the connection to the hub real and growing.

Second, as healthy Christians we need to grow interpersonally with brothers and sisters in Christ—that is, the support network of the inner rim. We must also grow in an obedient mission relationship toward our neighbor beyond the inner rim—in the world, where the outer rim contacts the road.

Third, each of the separate and unique spokes of our own individuality and giftedness needs to be creatively fulfilled. Each needs to develop and reach its own fullest level of potential. What are some of the unique spokes within your own life of which you are now aware? What do you think might be some of the others you have yet to discover? As I see it, the whole of Paul's teaching in 1 Corinthians 12, 13, and 14 has as its goal the Apostle's concern that the ordinary Christians at Corinth discover their uniqueness in Christ, their own giftedness, and then grow in that uniqueness to the glory of God and for the benefit of the other members of the body and the world.

The marvelous irony of Christian centralism, in which Jesus Christ is the center of our lives, is that with Christ as true center we are more free to be fully and uniquely ourselves than with any other center or combination of centers. Therefore let me warn you against any vision of the Christian church which would idealize the church as a community of identical people who all act alike, who look alike, or who are theologically and politically in lock-step with each other. There are many movements that feature such uniformity; if you were to punch a computer identity key for such a movement, a card would appear that completely defines the proper and approved member of that group—hair style, clothing style, political affiliation, doctrinal conviction on every point. There is no such ideal for the biblical Christian, and we must beware attempts to create such a model.

The truth is that, with Jesus Christ as center, the uniqueness spokes of our lives thrive, precisely because of the fact that Jesus Christ is not threatened by our individual potential. He is not diminished by either our intellectual discoveries or by our artistic accomplishments. Therefore, the gospel rejoices in our personal development—and that includes all intellectual, spiritual, and emotional breakthroughs. Every scientific and every artistic advance by a man or woman on this earth is, after all, an expression of the stewardship mandate (our responsibility to tend the earth) and the cultural mandate (our responsibility to rejoice at the wonder of God's design) that God has given to us.

Truth is never threatened by the eager, persistent search for truth. The glory of God is enhanced by the beauty of our music and art. God's glory inspires the arts and stirs them. And it is the careful order of creation that has given science its very character and promise. Science, philosophy, and theology share a common concern for reality, even though that shared journey has sometimes been a stormy one. The point is clear—the scientific mandate is an expression of the truth quest, and it was granted to men and women by God in the opening of the human story. Man was commanded by God to name the animals one by one. By this act, the science of biology was born, and with it philosophy as well. The careful classification and interpretation of data has from that time onward been at the core of the scientific method.

The Christian gospel is a profound stimulus to the growing mind. It is not honored by empty-headedness, and never has been. Therefore, all forms of anti-intellectualism are a denial of the stewardship mandate in Genesis and are against the will of God for our lives. What we really need is clearheadedness; we need growing, active minds that are in full pursuit of ideas and information. This is how the spiritual gifts of discernment are sharpened and enabled to have their vital Christian impact in the world of ideas.

It is because of this mandate that I as a Christian want to resist the twentieth-century chemical assault upon the brain—what G. K. Chesterton called "all dram drinking and every tendency to increase the dose." Stimulant, hallucinogenic, and depressant drugs are a major challenge to clearheadedness. Each of these additives has a blurring effect, one way or another, upon the mind. I believe they should be strongly resisted, even if this was their only danger. Add to this the other cumulative physical, genetic, and psychological dangers, and we see the full extent of the threat of drugs. But the argument against the chemical assault that is most compelling to me is the basic desire I have to keep my mind clear. God is not served better by the sleepy admiration of those who will not do the work to think, nor by a mind that staggers around in a fog of drugs—regardless of how "spiritually" exciting that fog may appear to the dedicated drug user.

Paul makes a very interesting point at the opening of the twelfth chapter of 1 Corinthians that relates to this question: ". . . you were led astray to dumb idols, however you may have been moved" (v. 2). The main argument of Paul in this sentence is that the crucial criterion for the Christian in the evaluation of all experiences is not the inspirational *feeling* of the experience, but rather the obedience of the experience to the true center, who is Jesus Christ. Paul readily agrees that there may be highly charged experiences that are in themselves deeply moving, but he warns that such inspirational experiences may in fact be idolatrous if they are not in obedience to the truth. Paul was not unaware that a famous first-century drug culture center was at Delphi, only a few miles from Corinth.

When the truth is at the center of our lives, there are many more interior and interpersonal experiences, and ones that have richer colors, than those which are artificially induced. When God created the world, he signaled his wealth to us in the intricate variety of all living things. Our redemption in Jesus Christ continues to endorse that exciting variety by the fact that in Christ we are given many different kinds of gifts which are all for the good of the body of Christ and the world. Another sign of God's richness is the wide divergence of personality types, cultural experiences, and racial backgrounds that are represented in the rim that we call the church. Because of this great reality, I do not find the fact that Christians often differ in questions of doctrine so much of a scandal. I agree with G. K. Chesterton that such debates in matters of doctrine are not necessarily a sign of weakness, but may in reality be the sign of health: "It was no flock of sheep the Christian Shepherd was leading, but a herd of bulls and tigers, of terrible ideals and devouring doctrines, each one of them strong enough to turn to a false religion and lay waste the world."[1]

The modern cultic phenomenon has produced movements in which there are no arguments about doctrine once the leader has spoken. In contrast, the earnestness and personal responsibility of the individual Christian disciple has always stimulated a concern on his or her part to search the Scriptures and see if doctrines are true. We must not confuse this divergence within the body of Christ with the factionalism about which Paul warns the Corinthians. On the one side, what we have in factionalism is a hardening of position into tight and confined people-controlled systems. On the other side, we have the earnest testing of all teaching by the standards of the Holy Scriptures. The one represents the closing off of the testing of doctrine, and it is that very feature which breaks up the peace, purity, and unity of the church. Arguments within a marriage are not scandalous; it is infidelity that is scandalous. The same principle is true in the Christian church:

Dogmatics is a critical science. So it cannot be held, as is sometimes thought, that it is a matter of stating certain old or even new propositions that one can take home in black and white. On the contrary, if there exists a critical science at all, which is constantly having to begin at the beginning, dogmatics is that science. Outwardly, of course, dogmatics arises from the fact that the Church's proclamation is in danger of going astray. Dogmatics is the testing of Church doctrine and proclamation, not an arbitrary testing from a freely chosen standpoint, but from the standpoint of the Church which in this case is the solely relevant standpoint. The concrete significance of this is that dogmatics measures the Church's proclamation by the standard of the Holy Scriptures, of the Old and New Testaments. Holy Scripture is the document of the manifestation of the Word of God in the person of Jesus Christ. We have no other document for this living basis of the Church; and where the Church is alive, it will always be having to reassess itself by this standard. We cannot pursue dogmatics without this standard being kept in sight. We must always be putting the question, "What is the evidence?" Not the evidence of my thoughts, or my heart, but the evidence of the apostles and prophets, as the evidence of God's self-evidence. Should a dogmatics lose sight of this standard, it would be an irrelevant dogmatics.[2]

8.

IMBALANCE

How does it happen that a man or woman who has known the true center should move away from that center toward the edges, toward false centers? How does the faith that was joyous and meaningful in the morning go stale in the afternoon? How does a Christian who serves and belongs to Jesus Christ as the true hub end up belonging to a religious or political leader, or a cultic movement? That was happening, or was beginning to happen, at Corinth, which is one reason Paul dashed off his first letter to the Christians in that city:

> For it has been reported to me by Chloe's people that there is quarreling among you, my brethren. What I mean is that each one of you says, "I belong to Paul," or "I belong to Apollos," or "I belong to Cephas," or "I belong to Christ." Is Christ divided? Was Paul crucified for you? Or were you baptized in the name of Paul (1 Cor. 1:11-13).

> For when one says, "I belong to Paul," and another, "I belong to Apollos," are you not merely men? What then is Apollos? What is Paul? Servants through whom you believed, as the Lord assigned to each. I planted, Apollos watered, but God gave the growth. So neither he who

plants nor he who waters is anything, but only God who gives the growth (1 Cor. 3:4–7).

This shift away from the center toward the edges was a problem in the first-century church and it is still a problem in the twentieth century. What sometimes happens is that a gradual shift takes place toward new starting points, new hubs with newly drawn circles around them. The new center may have a Christian origin, as in the case at Corinth, or the new starting point may be in fact totally separate and independent of any Christian origins; in this case, a new religion is being founded. But if the shift has occurred within the larger fellowship of faith, so that a new center is established apart from the triune center of Christian faith, then this shift away from center is the beginning of cultism in the church. Dietrich Bonhoeffer said it short and sweet: "We were meant to live from the center and not at the center." This affirmation is not only a warning regarding personal discipleship; it is also a warning to Christian movements.

The primary distinction between renewal movements within the church, which are healthy influences, and pre-

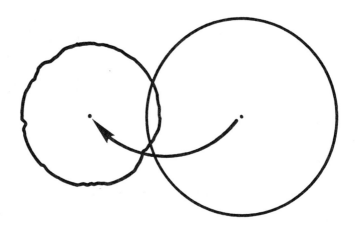

cultic and cultic movements at the edge of the church, which are destructive influences, is precisely at this point. A renewal movement is a concerned grouping of Christians who are at work on a weakness which they perceive within the rim. They care deeply about the health and integrity of that rim, but their center remains the true hub, and therefore they and their special concerns are under the check and balance of the rim itself. Even more vital, the authority of the center and the authoritative witness to that living center—the Bible—stands over the renewal movement. Every renewal or reformation movement within Christianity has welcomed this servant role. One such renewal fellowship was the "confessing church" movement in Germany during the Nazi era. Listen to the way in which these Christians expressed this essential sense of priority and obedience in the opening sentences of the Barmen Declaration of 1934:

> Try the Spirits whether they are of God! Prove also the words of the Confessional Synod of the German Evangelical Church to see whether they agree with Holy Scripture and with the confessions of the Fathers. If you find that we are speaking contrary to Scripture, then do not listen to us. . . . [1]

Cultic movements are quite a different matter. They may bear a resemblance to Christianity, and may share Christian teaching to a greater or lesser extent. But the essential difference is that a different starting point has been established; a shift away from the living center has taken place. Therefore it becomes impossible to test or challenge the concerns or teachings of the movement on the basis either of the church universal or of the authority of the biblical witness. The movement may save space for Jesus within the total program or doctrines of the new circle, but there is no way to call its leaders and their special doctrines into question, since the full authority of Jesus Christ and the written Word of God have been doctrinally shaken off by the new movement. This is cultism, and it offers its followers a special and destructive form of freedom from the church universal, from the Bible, and from Christ himself—a kind of freedom which exerts a strong attraction to certain individuals. The leader in such a movement is "free" to develop elaborate and specialized doctrines which may appear ideally relevant to the felt needs of people and the moods of a particular historical setting.

The questions we must now ask are these: How does such a shift away from center occur? What happens within the new subcircles? What are the cures for those who become involved in a cultic subcircle?

First, how does the shift occur? Why would a Corinthian, for instance, move onto this outward pathway away from the largeness and truth of the gospel toward the narrowing subcircle of the Apollos group or the Peter group or the Paul group? I believe there may be several reasons. One reason is disappointment with the church. This disappointment motivates some Christians to join forces with renewal movements in order to heal the church. But that same disappointment causes others to despair of the rim, the spokes, and finally of the hub. They reach out toward what they think will be a new program, a new beginning, a new leader. The shift is an afternoon attempt to defy the staleness that has set in. A second reason is the positive and attractive appeal of the new movement and its leadership; gifted and decisive leadership always draws people. Finally, there are new doctrines and interpretations and claims. A new gospel with a different message can win people away from the true center because of the appearance of freshness or the promise of a different breakthrough.

The question now is this: What happens to a movement

once it establishes its separate effective starting point and attracts followers? There are four developments that usually follow, though the intensity will vary from case to case.

First, there is a tendency toward the establishment of absolute centralized leadership. This "guru" phenomenon has been observed in all subcircle movements. Second, there is an inevitable pressure toward doctrinal specialization. The distinctive points of the movement become increasingly essential for recruitment of new followers and for the justification of the movement. Therefore, those themes which at best would have deserved secondary status in the beginning of the movement eventually become its celebrated proud towers.

A third development that emerges within the subcircle movement is the narrowing process. The subcircle reinforces its own fellowship experience by the claim to exclusiveness, so that as time passes the movement becomes increasingly sure that it and it alone is the faithful fellowship, while all others are deviant. The criterion for this judgment is the specialized doctrine of the movement, and the result is a narrow, self-serving, "inner circle" mentality.

The fourth development has to do with ethics, and will often result in grave harm. Self-conceived, self-authenticating, self-governing movements develop a tendency toward a self-justifying ethical stance toward the world. This stance will allow for ethical shortcuts in relation to outsiders. Just as the most dangerous person is that person who perceives himself or herself as without fault, in the same way a movement that is not itself under the law and the gospel will be strongly tempted toward ethical ruthlessness. An "ends justify means" ethic is very plausible if the goal is to further the purposes and grand design of the movement.

This form of shortcut ethic was strongly advocated

within the revolutionary philosophy of dialectical materialism. The argument of Marx and Lenin was that whatever action which stirs up the struggle between classes in a bourgeois society is "good," because such struggle "must" bring on revolution, and out of revolution comes the new synthesis of justice for the masses. Such an ethic is unencumbered by any outside criteria. We have witnessed the cruel and dehumanizing result of this subjugation of ethics under the revolutionary motif of Leninist Marxism. Alexander Solzhenitsyn opens his terrifying book, *The Gulag Archipelago*, with the narrative of the brutal repression of ordinary Russian citizens by the Soviet government from the time of Lenin to the 1950s. He tells of the waves of arrests and the imprisonment of millions of people. There was no defense against the arrests, authorized by Lenin as the "merciless suppression of attempts at anarchy on the part of drunkards, hooligans, counter-revolutionaries, and other persons," and carried out by all agencies of the government, especially the *cheka*, or secret police, "the only punitive organ in human history that combined in one set of hands investigation, arrest, interrogation, prosecution, trial, and execution of the verdict."[2]

But this form of ethical short-cutting has not been limited to Lenin's brand of Marxism. It has characterized political movements of both the extreme right and of the extreme left. Its premise has been used to justify both terrorism and repression. When there is no outside restraint upon the authority of the ruling cadre, when leadership claims an absolute authority beyond the check and balance of any other criteria, the result is often tyranny and bloodshed.

These four developments which can be observed in a precultic or cultic movement may also occur within Christian fellowship, and such tragic developments, when they have occurred, have scarred the witness of the church. The difference is that within biblical faith every single believer is encouraged to test the faith and the life of the fellowship by the standard of Holy Scripture (Acts 17:11). It is this process of testing that allows for and enables the possibility of renewal and reform without disintegrating into cultism. A cultic movement does not encourage this same vigorous access to the Bible or to any outside authority; therefore the fellowship becomes too obedient to too small a starting point.

There are short-term advantages that accompany each of the four developments that characterize a cultic movement, but there are even greater long-term dangers. These characteristics are marks of imbalance, and they produce a bitter fruit of arrogance and isolation. Paul knew that these dangers would inevitably confront the Christians at Corinth, because of the tentative break-up they were experiencing. His urgency, and his appeal at the opening of his correspondence to the Corinthian church, was rooted in his deep concern about the precultic scenario he observed at Corinth.

His approach was typically fresh and direct. He named names, called out the warning, resigned from the group that had apparently centered itself around his name. Then he points the Corinthians all toward the true and living Center—the cure for imbalance both in the church and in individual lives.

9.

THE CHALLENGE OF LEGALISM

There are three major cultic challenges to the Christian faith that Paul grapples with in his letters to the Corinthians. If we put it another way, we might describe these as three different kinds of imbalance in the wheel. Let me identify these three as follows: the legalistic imbalance, the spiritualistic imbalance, and the apocalyptic imbalance. During the formation of the Christian church in the first century each of these three imbalances posed a serious threat to the young churches. The challenge sometimes came singly, but more often came in combinations of all three. Every letter in the New Testament grapples with these three principal forms of false teaching, and some of the most decisive examples of that grappling are to be found in Paul's two letters to the Corinthians.

Today, in the late twentieth century, the dangers of cultism are still as real as they were in Paul's age, and what becomes clear as we study the first-century situation is that what looks like a new development to us is really very old. The imbalance of cultism represented today by legalistic, spiritualistic, apocalyptic movements have their philosophical and theological roots in the same false starting points that confronted the New Testament churches of

Paul, John, and Peter. The leaders of present movements are twentieth-century personalities, and the vocabulary is sometimes twentieth-century vocabulary, but the basic ideas at the heart of the movements are usually very old ideas.

Therefore, in the light of this continuity, it will be very important for us today to understand the cultic challenges to healthy biblical Christian faith that were present in the first century. We need this historical perspective in order to dialogue realistically and helpfully with people who are caught up in the movements we encounter in the twentieth century.

Let us first consider the legalistic imbalance that confronted the first-century Christians. Paul's letter to the Galatians is almost totally devoted to the problems of legalism which had harmed the Christian fellowship in Galatia! He appealed to the wayward Christians at Galatia to return from the legalistic edges and to once again embrace the liberating center: "For freedom Christ has set us free; stand fast therefore, and do not submit again to a yoke of slavery" (Gal. 5:1).

Most of the legalistic distortions that we meet in the New Testament were not so extreme or so hardened as to be described as cultic. The churches Paul addressed his letters to had not shifted from the central authority of Jesus Christ as Lord and Savior. Therefore, the apostle was more concerned about a low-grade drift toward legalism than about a dramatic break. It was legalism's gradual distortion of the centered wheel that alarmed Paul.

We note Paul's concern about this legalistic drift in 1 and 2 Corinthians. His approach to the people at Corinth caught up in the Galatian-type legalism was to show how the law of Moses itself was fulfilled in Jesus Christ. This passage includes some of Paul's most brilliant writing:

Now if the dispensation of death, carved in letters on stone, came with such splendor that the Israelites could not look at

Moses' face because of its brightness, fading as this was, will not the dispensation of the Spirit be attended with greater splendor? For if there was splendor in the dispensation of condemnation, the dispensation of righteousness must far exceed it in splendor. Indeed, in this case, what once had splendor has come to have no splendor at all, because of the splendor that surpasses it. For if what faded away came with splendor, what is permanent must have much more splendor.

Since we have such a hope, we are very bold, not like Moses, who put a veil over his face so that the Israelites might not see the end of the fading splendor. But their minds were hardened; for to this day, when they read the old covenant, that same veil remains unlifted, because only through Christ is it taken away. Yes, to this day whenever Moses is read a veil lies over their minds; but when a man turns to the Lord the veil is removed. Now the Lord is the Spirit, and where the Spirit of the Lord is, there is freedom. And we all, with unveiled face, beholding the glory of the Lord, are being changed into his likeness from one degree of glory to another; for this comes from the Lord who is the Spirit (2 Cor. 3:7–18).

But even though legalism in the New Testament churches had not reached cultic levels, legalism *can* become cultic. The deterioration toward legalistic cultism in Christian fellowships happens as the center shifts from the fulfillment of law as found in Jesus Christ toward the performance of law. In this case, what happens is that an individual's confidence and meaning become grounded in himself or herself, and in his or her own proof of piety, which varies from legalism to legalism. The proof might consist in one movement of the satisfaction of particular ritual, or in another movement of concrete ethical performance. Whether the proof is extreme or moderate, the principle is still the same: *the individuals and the movement become their own gospel.* The gospel is not based on Christ's adequacy and his sovereign love, but on human adequacy and proofs of piety. The legalistic movement affirms its own devotion and acts of devotion as the good word. The result is a steady erosion of hope.

The temptation of legalistic cultism, by which a biblical Christian is drawn away from a Christocentric faith, may sound something like this: "Your faith in Christ is fine so far as it goes, but it is not concrete enough." The cultic movement makes roughly the following argument: "Join with our movement because we can specify concrete, definite works that prove our superiority to your nominal faith in Christ." Following this theological-discipleship claim, the legalistic movement then offers its own definite, special acts that constitute the proof of its superiority to the inadequate faith of ordinary Christians.

In the case of the Galatian challengers, that specific concrete proof was the rite of circumcision performed as a sign of the full obedience to the law of Moses. Twentieth-century legalistic cultism offers different specific proofs. A movement of the left might argue as follows: "Yes, you believe in Jesus Christ, but can you prove your real faith with these qualifying acts which our movement has decreed are the acts of the Spirit in the world today? Are you involved in the battle for liberation, and against the economic oppression of imperialism . . . ?" Rightist legalistic movements of our generation would develop the identical theological heresy, but with a different choice of concrete act: "Yes, you believe in Jesus Christ, but can you prove your real faith with the qualifying acts which our movement has decreed are the acts of the Spirit in the world today? Are you against the economic and social oppression of communism . . . ?" The list of particular concerns is widely divergent from legalistic movement to legalistic movement, but the starting point is the same—whether the movement is rightist or leftist, concerned with religious concrete acts or with ethical concrete acts.

It is the starting point that distinguishes a cultic movement from a reform-renewal movement. The question we must always ask is this: Is the movement under primary obedience to the biblical witness to the living Center—who is Jesus Christ, or is the movement for all practical purposes independent of that central obedience? If the movement holds fast to the true center, it is not cultic but stands and works in the great tradition of the reform movements of the books of James and Philemon and Revelation. This means its leaders and its doctrines are not beyond the check and balance of the witness of the Holy Spirit and the biblical witness. Any Christian has the right, and indeed the solemn responsibility, to test every movement, its leadership and its doctrines, on the basis of the witness of the Word of God. Where this check and balance is not possible, where Jesus Christ as Lord is not spiritually, intellectually, and morally central; then the movement has drifted off-center, has made for itself a new hub and drawn up a new rim.

Because the acts associated with a movement—either ethical or religious or social—are sometimes very impressive at the first glance; there is often an intense drawing power for the people who see these works. I had a conversation a year ago with a young man who had been drawn to a certain movement in Berkeley. He told me, "You know, they are really very sincere, they really know how to love, they are clean-cut, and they help people." He told me of cases he knew of individuals caught up in drugs being helped by this group to shake their lives out of the grip of drugs. But he still had an uneasy feeling about the group, and finally he said to me, "I think that 90 percent of their teaching is really great, but about 10 percent is off the wall." I asked him what he felt the 10 percent was. He said, "They have some strange ideas about Jesus Christ." During the remainder of our conversation we explored together this deadly 10 percent. It turns out that the 10 percent had to do with the center, and was more significant by far than the impressive social concerns and sincerity of the 90 percent.

That in no way discounts the good work a cultic movement may do in aiding individuals. Christians would do well to be challenged by the social concern of such a movement to examine our motivations and our lifestyles before God, and to open up our hands to do the work the love of Jesus Christ calls us to do. We do right to be challenged by every movement around us, and in fact that has been the case throughout history. For instance, Martin Luther battled intellectually against the scholar John Eck during the formative days of the Reformation. John Eck and Luther stood at opposite poles in their dialogue. Nevertheless, Luther was grateful for the debate, and he acknowledged, "Dr. Eck made me wide awake."

However, even though the deadly 10 percent can be a healthy challenge to us, it is still deadly, and that fact makes the all-important difference. Adolf Hitler and the social reforms of national socialism built the *autobahn* and put the idle youth to work in Germany, but that social service did not qualify him for the adoration and obedience he demanded from the German people. The history of social movements shows that, without the profoundly good center that comes from the word and work of God himself, even the good acts of legalistic movements turn arrogant and finally destructive, because they are not meaningfully framed within a larger context. Good works especially must receive their true motivation and limitation from the law and gospel. John put it this way: "We love others because he first loved us." When a person who is trying to serve and love severs the relationship from the One who first loved, the result is always the loss of the true reason for love and at last the power to love.

10.

SPIRITUALISM

There is another imbalance that is at the opposite swing of the pendulum from legalism. Whereas legalism emphasizes concrete proof of piety, this imbalance emphasizes the spiritual proof of piety. Its argument might sound something like this: "Your faith in Jesus Christ is fine *so far as it goes*, but it is not spiritual enough." In the face of this argument the Christian is ashamed because of a lack of spiritual breakthroughs, a lack of experience with mystical depth. Spiritualistic movements have promises to make about secret discoveries and powers which are available to those who fulfill the necessary conditions.

There is agreement among most New Testament scholars that it is a spiritualistic imbalance that most troubled the Corinthian Christians. As we read closely the two letters of Paul to the Corinthians, we are able to discover some of the features of this imbalance. Certain teachers at Corinth had persuaded a number of people in the church that there were profound spiritual breakthroughs to be experienced, but not as long as the Corinthians stayed bound to the slow-moving message of Paul. These teachers claimed that the message of Paul was the condescending message for beginners, but that now the Corinthians should move ahead to the richer and fuller truths Paul had failed to teach them. We see this charge behind the words Paul uses:

> When I came to you, brethren, I did not come proclaiming to you the testimony of God in lofty words or wisdom. For I decided to know nothing about you except Jesus Christ and him crucified. And I was with you in weakness and in much fear and trembling; and my speech and my message were not in plausible words of wisdom, but in demonstration of the Spirit and power, that your faith might not rest in the wisdom of men but in the power of God (1 Cor. 2:1–5).

These teachers at Corinth sought to prove their point by a personal attack upon Paul himself. They suggested that he was mentally confused (note 2 Cor. 5:11–15). They suggested that Paul had not experienced the highest breakthrough of special mystical tongues and miraculous discoveries (note Paul's reply to this charge in 2 Cor. 6:3–10). They also charged that Paul's inability to receive physical healing for his illness was proof of his spiritual inadequacy. Paul's answer to this most brutal of the charges against him contains some of the most dramatic teaching upon the true meaning of the gospel in all of the New Testament: "When I am weak, then I am strong" (1 Cor. 12:10).

From the evidence in the letters of Paul we conclude that the spiritualistic imbalance at Corinth involved a fascination with mystery and mystical experiences, with healings, and with the discovery of deeper truths. The people who were caught up in this new wave at Corinth also believed that the fact of their higher spiritual development necessarily transported them beyond the more basic truths about the gospel of the cross of Christ. They were offended by Paul's continual insistence upon that message of repentance and salvation in Christ. In their mind they had graduated from the beginners' school and were now at a graduate level.

Another result they claimed from their new spiritual achievement was a freedom from all moral restraint of the law and gospel. These new-wave "spiritual" Corinthians were sternly challenged by Paul throughout his two letters for what he called a faulty understanding of freedom (note 1 Cor. 10:31–11:1). Later in the first century, the Gnostic movements held some of the same views as we found in this initial formation in the Corinthian church. Then the church father Irenaeas challenged these Gnostic spiritualists, just as Paul had done earlier:

> ... Certain men, rejecting the truth, are introducing among us false stories and vain genealogies, which serve rather to controversies, as the apostle said, than to God's work of building up in the faith. By their craftily constructed rhetoric they lead astray the minds of the inexperienced, and take them captive, corrupting the oracles of the Lord, and being evil expounders of what was well spoken. For they upset many, leading them away by the pretense of knowledge from Him who constituted and ordered the universe, as if they had something higher and greater to show them than the God who made the heaven and the earth and all that is in them.[1]

But although he is concerned about the misinterpretation of freedom, Paul is even more distressed about the new-wave Corinthians' faulty understanding of what is truly central. This theological concern is what dominates Paul's letters to the Corinthians, because in the apostle's mind the great danger in spiritualistic imbalance is the subtle shift away from true center and toward the exotic and inspirational experiences which the leaders at Corinth were beginning to treasure more than they did Christ himself.

Like the Corinthian variety, twentieth-century spiritualistic cultism insists that ordinary and mere Christian faith is not spiritual enough in and of itself, without special breakthroughs. It is just this sort of entrance into deeper experience that is offered by the movement. It makes its appeal to the human appetite for *more,* and in union with that appetite it creates the heresy of "hyper":

> The Corinthians' preoccupation with what they under-stood as the spiritual remedy, namely the remarkable and the powerful, lifted them above... the common lot of be-lievers in the church.... The Corinthian letters are a sus-tained attempt to formulate what Luther later called a *theologia crucis,* a theology of the cross. God's way of work-ing in the world—to men an inefficient way, and thus a proof of its divinity—is the way of weakness. The crucified Christ himself is this way's classic content; the cross its classic form; the struggling church (and church member) its classic sphere.[2]

The results of spiritual cultism are far-reaching, both within the lives and attitudes of the converts to this form of cultism, and also in the theological redefinition that must take place in order to sustain the claims of spiritualism.

First consider the theological fallout. Spiritualistic cult-ism must redefine Jesus Christ. The person who is drawn toward the Gnostic world of spiritualism is taught new ways of viewing Jesus. Jesus is sometimes treated as a physical representation of a greater mystery. This means that the really important constant is the secret of the mys-tery, and that its historical representation can vary. There-fore, once an initiate into such a movement has discovered the secret, then the need for Jesus is diminished, just as any accidental incident of history diminishes in impor-tance once its significance is decoded. It is the fallacy of this premise that Paul challenges in his electrifying introduc-tion to his teaching on spiritual gifts and the mystical body of Christ:

> Now concerning spiritual gifts, brethren, I do not want you to be uninformed. You know that when you were heathen, you were led astray to dumb idols, however you may have

been moved. Therefore I want you to understand that no one speaking by the Spirit of God ever says "Jesus be cursed!" and no one can say "Jesus is Lord" except by the Holy Spirit (1 Cor. 12:1-3).

Paul is fully aware that mystical experiences may be impressive, but he warns the Corinthians that the ministry of the Holy Spirit will always draw the believer *toward Jesus Christ as Lord,* and never toward a devaluation of Christ as word and event. What Jesus said is inseparable from what Jesus did. His act and being are one, and that is the mystery beyond which no greater mystery awaits.

Another form of redefinition of Jesus Christ interprets him as a stage or doorway in a vast spiritual journey through which the believer must pass but then proceed on toward still greater doorways. In this view Christ is treated as one who only partially completed his kingdom mission. The argument continues that now, in this later and more advanced age, it is the task of later door openers to complete an unfinished work. Paul rejects this interpretation with two thrilling sentences: "From now on, therefore, we regard no one from a human point of view; even though we once regarded Christ from a human point of view, we regard him thus no longer. Therefore, if any one is in Christ, he is a new creation; the old has passed away, behold, the new has come" (2 Cor. 5:16, 17).

A third form of redefinition is both the most ancient and the most dangerous. In this view, the person of Christ himself is recast into a totally spiritual revelation, so that his actual humanity and physical identification with humanity is denied. The Jesus Christ of this third redefinition is treated as a pure spirit. He only appeared to be human; he only appeared to die upon the cross. His human likeness was a phantom-like appearance of the common and the earthly. He is like the mystical seagull in Richard Bach's *Jonathan Livingston Seagull:* "A limitless number... an unlimited idea."[3]

But the Jesus we meet in the New Testament is real. His identification with humanity is total and therefore Paul, like John ("For many deceivers have gone into the world, men who will not acknowledge the coming of Jesus Christ in the flesh; such a one is the deceiver and the antichrist"— 2 John 7) stands fast on this issue against the attempts to spiritualize first Jesus Christ and then us: "I decided to know nothing among you except Jesus Christ and Him crucified" (1 Cor. 2:2).

In each of these redefinitions, Jesus Christ is downgraded. In each interpretation, the lion is tamed, and the mystery to which the particular movement has privileged access is glorified. In each case, our need of Jesus as Savior and Lord is also downgraded. In his place, a new need is announced and a new promise is offered. The need is for the discovery of the hidden secret or clue so that we might enter into harmony with the spiritual flow of the eternal. To answer this new need, a secret—not the Savior—is offered.

On the surface, these spiritualistic promises appear to honor the human personality with the soaring offer of spiritual achievement and fulfillment. But in fact, as the concrete and historical importance of Jesus is reduced, the concrete significance of us as human beings also suffers reduction. If Jesus was not real in any sense that I can relate to from the standpoint of my planet-earth existence, then I have no guarantee of my own reality or worth.

During the first three centuries of the life of the church, the primitive church was in continuous struggle with Gnostic movements which represented the spiritualistic, cultic challenge to the gospel in that crucial time of the church. This controversy forced the Christian church to really think through the central questions of the gospel, and Christians throughout the centuries have benefited from this examination. The Nicaean Creed of the fourth century was the affirmation of conscience and faith that resulted from those years of contest:

I believe in one God,
the Father Almighty,
maker of heaven and earth,
and of all things visible and invisible;

And in one Lord Jesus Christ,
the only-begotten Son of God,
begotten of his Father before all worlds,
God of God, Light of Light,
very God of very God,
begotten, not made,
being of one substance with the Father;
by whom all things were made;
who for us men and for our salvation came down from
heaven,
and was incarnate by the Holy Ghost of the Virgin Mary,
and was made man;
and was crucified also for us under Pontius Pilate;
he suffered and was buried;
and the third day he rose again according to the Scriptures,
and ascended into heaven,
and sitteth on the right hand of the Father;
and he shall come again, with glory, to judge both
the quick and the dead;
whose kingdom shall have no end.

And I believe in the Holy Ghost the Lord, and Giver of Life,
who proceedeth from the Father and the Son;
who with the Father and the Son together is worshiped
and glorified;
who spake by the Prophets.
And I believe in one holy Catholic and Apostolic Church;
I acknowledge one Baptism for the remission of sins;
and I look for the resurrection of the dead, and the
life of the world to come. Amen.[4]

Gnosticism, as it spiritualizes both Christ and man,
erodes every basis for ethics and the realistic understanding of personhood. Listen to the ancient Church father

Irenaeus as he describes the Gnostic point of view: "If one should read over all their creedal statements, he would find that they always bring in the Word of God and the Christ who is from above as without flesh and free from suffering."[5] This is why the spiritualistic movements from those early days until our own time have tended to be escapist and unrealistic. When suffering and flesh are denied, then the very foundation of all human experience is set adrift. For example, it is very difficult to come up with useful and healthy guidelines for the understanding of our sexual nature if the starting premise is that human sexuality is itself only apparently real, with no concrete and essential significance. If only the spiritual is real, then how do we understand our emotions, our physical suffering, our sinfulness, our oppression? Gnosticism was not able to come up with any whole or total solutions to these kinds of questions, because the Gnostic man or woman has already mentally taken leave of the earth.

But the Bible never discounts or rebukes the earth for its seasons or we human beings for our humanity. The biblical hope is not the absorption of spirit into eternity but the resurrection of the body. It is the whole of what we are as persons that God loves, and that alone is reason enough for Paul to reject the nonsense of spiritualism:

> For the love of Christ controls us, because we are convinced that one has died for all; therefore all have died. And he died for all, that those who live might live no longer for themselves but for him who for their sake died and was raised (2 Cor. 5:14-15).

The reason still stands today.

11.

THE CULTISM OF FEAR

There is a third cultic challenge to the balance of the wheel, and I will describe this as the cultism of fear. This cultism attacks the Christian's faith with a line of reasoning that may sound something like this: "Your faith in Jesus Christ is fine so far as it goes, but it is not strong enough in the face of the dangers of our time." The promise that the cultism of fear then offers is the promise of special protection and power for those who submit to the movement and its survivalist doctrines.

We are able to demonstrate in the study of the Corinthian letters, of the second letter to Timothy, and also of 1 and 2 Thessalonians that this form of cultism had attacked the faith of the early Christians. The precise teaching of the first-century form of the cultism of fear went as follows: they claimed that, though Jesus Christ had won his own victory over death in his resurrection, it does not follow that Christ's victory means victory over death and over the devil for his disciples. Death is too great a foe for that, and therefore newer remedies are needed to conquer death and the cosmic evil forces that hold power in company with death.

Paul takes on this teaching in his very first letters—the

letters to the Thessalonians—and also in his final letter—
the letter to Timothy (see 2 Tim. 2:17–19). But it is in 1 and
2 Corinthians that Paul writes most forcefully in response
to this false teaching. The fifteenth chapter of 1 Corinthians is a brilliant and clear statement by Paul against this
form of the cultism of fear:

> Now if Christ is preached as raised from the dead, how can
> some of you say that there is no resurrection of the dead?
> But if there is no resurrection of the dead, then Christ has
> not been raised; if Christ has not been raised, then our
> preaching is in vain and your faith is in vain. We are even
> found to be misrepresenting God, because we testified of
> God that he raised Christ, whom he did not raise if it is true
> that the dead are not raised. For if the dead are not raised,
> then Christ has not been raised. If Christ has not been
> raised, your faith is futile and you are still in your sins. Then
> those also who have fallen asleep in Christ have perished. If
> for this life only we have hoped in Christ, we are of all men
> most to be pitied (1 Cor. 15:12–19).

He closes this chapter with a very moving, positive,
statement of hope:

> Lo! I tell you a mystery. We shall not all sleep, but we shall
> all be changed, in a moment, in the twinkling of an eye, at
> the last trumpet. For the trumpet will sound, and the dead
> will be raised imperishable, and we shall be changed. For
> this perishable nature must put on the imperishable, and
> this mortal nature must put on immortality. When the per-
> ishable puts on the imperishable, and the mortal puts on
> immortality, then shall come to pass the saying that is writ-
> ten:
>
> "Death is swallowed up in victory.
> O death, where is thy victory?
> O death, where is thy sting?"

The sting of death is sin, and the power of sin is the law. But thanks be to God, who gives us the victory through our Lord Jesus Christ. Therefore, my beloved brethren, be steadfast, immovable, always abounding in the work of the Lord, knowing that in the Lord your labor is not in vain (1 Cor. 15:51–58).

If the cultism of fear is to make its case believable, it must convince its would-be followers of two things: first, that the dangers of death and the dangers of evil are cosmic and human and more ominous than they really are, and second, that the gospel of Jesus Christ as Lord and Savior is weaker than these dangers.

This teaching becomes cultic precisely at the point that it loses confidence in the lordship of Jesus Christ, so that the gospel is treated as if it were inadequate for the especially acute present dangers that confront humanity—the reality of death, and the reality of the devil. But this sense of fright and panic is foreign to the Bible. The Old and New Testaments are always realistic about death, and about all forms of evil, but without the hysterical reflex which lies at the motivational core of the cultisms of fear. Death is never taken lightly in either the Old Testament or New Testament. Death is the foe. For this reason, suicide is always treated as sin in the Bible; it is the sin against all life. It mocks life as if death were better: "It is the refusal to take an interest in life. The man who kills a man, kills a man. The man who kills himself, kills all men."[1]

The biblical view of both life and death is realistic and wholistic. And biblical hope is not a denial of the reality of death (as is the case with Greek immortality teaching), but rather the shout of victory over death.

We as Christians do not believe that we are immortal in the sense that we cannot die. Our basis for hope is that, because of the actual victory of Jesus Christ over the real death he faced in our behalf, there is an actual and concrete victory over death for us, too. Our hope is the hope of resurrection, which means that death is not explained away or dreamed away, but disarmed of its final power by the one who went through its valley from one end to the other. Because of Christ's victory, and for that reason alone, the Christian is neither preoccupied and fascinated with death nor in dread of its power. Paul expresses his own outlook with these words:

> For we know that if the earthly tent we live in is destroyed, we have a building from God, a house not made with hands, eternal in the heavens. Here indeed we groan, and long to put on our heavenly dwelling, so that by putting it on we may not be found naked. For while we are still in this tent, we sigh with anxiety; not that we would be unclothed, but that we would be further clothed, so that what is mortal may be swallowed up by life. He who has prepared us for this very thing is God, who has given us the Spirit as a guarantee. So we are always of good courage; we know that while we are at home in the body we are away from the Lord, for we walk by faith, not by sight. We are of good courage, and we would rather be away from the body and at home with the Lord. So whether we are at home or away, we make it our aim to please him. For we must all appear before the judgment seat of Christ, so that each one may receive good or evil, according to what he has done in the body (2 Cor. 5:1–10).

As for the problems of evil, the biblical world-view is equally realistic. The Bible recognizes the existence of a cosmic and personal will that strives against the will of God—the devil (see the discussion of the biblical understanding of the devil in E. F. Palmer's Commentary on Revelation[2]). The existence of the devil is a reality because by God's decision there exists a freedom at the cosmic level of existence, just as there exists freedom at the human level.

The freedom at the cosmic level makes it possible for the
devil to exist, just as freedom at the human level makes
human evil a possibility and reality. But freedom also
makes possible love, faith, and hope!

The real questions are: How much power does evil have
in both of its forms—cosmic and human? What kind of
power does evil have, and are there limits upon that
power? The answer to these questions will have a crucial
influence on whether a person is a candidate for the alarming message of the many cultisms of fear that challenge
our own generation today.

The biblical answer is clear. Human sins are garden-
variety sins, and they always have been. The sins of today
are not generically different from the sins of previous gen-
erations. Idolatry is still idolatry, even though the idols
sometimes change with the fads and seasons of culture;
spiritual pride remains pride, regardless of the century.
Human sins do real harm to the people around us, to
ourselves, and to the earth; they always have. But the sins
of today are not more powerful or more difficult to heal
than they were at the time of our Lord, the time of Genghis
Khan, or the time of the California Gold Rush.

The vital theological truth to remember is this—human
sin has always been bounded by the decision of God.
God's judgment is a boundary, and there is no human sin
that is beyond the boundary of the righteous judgment of
God. In the good news of Jesus Christ, we have also discovered the radical interruption within the boundary,
which is the surprise of God's forgiveness and love. There
is no human sin that cannot be forgiven, except for one
alone—and that is rejection of God's forgiveness. God's
respect for the dignity of our freedom requires that this
one doorway remain fixed in the boundary of forgiveness.
That one doorway does not increase the damage human sin
is able to do to others or to the earth, but only the damage
to the self that walks through it. All other wickedness and

wrath, all violence and terror, is bounded by God's judgment. There is no such thing as runaway sin that races beyond God's eternal boundary. The gospel believes in this fact, and that is why Paul is not reduced to hysteria and panic by persecution or the human sin that lies behind it. Listen to the apostle:

> But we have this treasure in earthen vessels, to show that the transcendent power belongs to God and not to us. We are afflicted in every way, but not crushed; perplexed, but not driven to despair; persecuted, but not forsaken; struck down but not destroyed; always carrying in the body the death of Jesus, so that the life of Jesus may also be manifested in our bodies. For while we live we are always being given up to death for Jesus' sake, so that the life of Jesus may be manifested in our mortal flesh. So death is at work in us, but life in you (2 Cor. 4:7–12).

Paul has the confidence in the ability of God to heal harmful sinfulness, and this confidence makes the main difference:

> For our sake he made him to be sin who knew no sin, so that in him we might become the righteousness of God. Working together with him, then, we entreat you not to accept the grace of God in vain. For he says, "At the acceptable time I have listened to you, and helped you on the day of salvation." Behold, now is the acceptable time; behold, now is the day of salvation (2 Cor. 5:21–6:2).

Paul does not make light of the contest we must be engaged in against the devil, but his one-line affirmation in Romans 16 shows his own conviction concerning the outcome of the contest: "Then the God of peace will soon crush Satan under your feet" (v. 20). In other words, the power of cosmic evil is bounded by the sovereign decision of God. The devil is the deceiver and the destroyer and the accuser, as he always has been, but there is a limitation on, a boundary around, his power. His deceptive purposes, then, are served by those who inflate the power he does have as well as by those who wishfully imagine he has no power: "There are two equal and opposite errors into which our race can fall about the devils. One is to disbelieve in their existence. The other is to believe, and to feel an excessive and unhealthy interest in them."[3]

Once the authority of Jesus Christ is displaced by the fear of danger, then the cultism of fear is able to prescribe its own cures and to exact its own price from the frightened people who now turn in desperation toward the promises of power. What happens next is the replacement of the joy and generous openness of the gospel with the search for enemies and a low-grade paranoia—a siege mentality. In the end, the person who is caught up in a steady emphasis of dread and preparedness for attack becomes brittle and angry. The anger is at first projected outward, toward those whom the movement has designated as enemies. But after awhile, the anger is directed toward God, for his supposed inadequacy in the face of the windstorms of fears the cultic movement itself has nurtured.

Those who have made a careful study of twentieth-century cultic movements will recognize that most movements in our century have taken on features of all three basic kinds of cultism. There is the promise of power, the promise of mystery, and the promise of pragmatic results. But Paul's counsel still has the ring of truth in the face of these unbalanced movements:

> Let no one deceive himself. If any one among you thinks that he is wise in this age, let him become a fool that he may become wise. For the wisdom of this world is folly with God. For it is written, "He catches the wise in their craftiness," and again, "The Lord knows that the thoughts of the

wise are futile." So let no one boast of men. For all things are yours, whether Paul or Apollos or Cephas or the world or life or death or the present or the future, all are yours; and you are Christ's; and Christ is God's (1 Cor. 3:18–23).

12.

THE WAY BACK

I have been a pastor of the First Presbyterian Church of Berkeley for twelve years. Our congregation worships at the very edge of the University of California campus. Our city is a windswept city—not only with the morning and evening fog from San Francisco Bay, but also with every kind of social, political, and religious movement. Some of these have been Christian renewal and reformation movements that have been born and nourished in Berkeley, and they have had significant influence for good throughout the whole church. But Berkeley has also been an originating center or developing ground for several of the cultic movements that have posed such a serious challenge to society as a whole and also to the Christian church. I have watched some of these movements very closely during these past twelve years, and I have talked with many people who have been involved in them. It is not my purpose in this chapter to identify any particular movement, but rather to examine the philosophical and theological themes, arguments, and motivations that lie at the core of many of these movements.

The three forms of cultic challenge that we have examined at first-century Corinth have their counterparts in this century and, as I have stated earlier, often one single movement will contain features of all three. The logic of terror, and survivalism with its brooding pessimism, may be united with the zealous obedience orientation of legalism as well as the spiritualistic theme of mystery and secret revelations. We today must face the challenge of the street and airport cult recruiters and their arguments, just as first-century Christians were forced to face up to the challenges of Gnosticism, legalism, and the theology of fear in the Mediterranean world. I believe the New Testament approach to these movements and to the people who are often deceived by them is very helpful and relevant to us today. The best cure I know for false doctrine is a healthy exposure to the narratives and letters of the New Testament.

The pastoral advice of Paul to the Corinthians was sensitive to the complexity of the crisis of faith they were facing, and also took a whole-person approach toward those who had become involved in cultism. At the heart of his letters, Paul invited the Corinthians to come into the larger hope of the gospel, rather than to become entangled in the intricate line-by-line disputation of the false arguments. This does not mean that Paul evaded particular issues, however. He was personal and interpersonal; he was bold; he clearly disclaimed any intent of becoming the guru of the "Paul" faction at Corinth. He was direct; in places he scolded the fellowship, but there was never any doubt about his love for the people to whom he wrote.

As we have seen, the one organizing clue to Paul's approach toward the Corinthians was his continuous affirmation and argument for the Center—Jesus Christ. It is as if Paul realized that the only fact he had which was itself strong and true and good enough to reform and renew his old friends in their Corinthian afternoon was the fact of the living Lord Jesus Christ who had first won them in the morning.

In the remainder of this book I want to consider with you some of the basic principles that undergird the approach of the Christian toward cultic movements, and especially toward the human beings who for one reason or many are presently a part of these movements. And in this chapter, particularly, I want to examine what we as Christians must do to keep ourselves on center—because I believe the answer to cultism begins with ourselves and with our own community of faith. We need to ask ourselves: is my own faith centered upon the true hub? Or have I substituted some other concern or mission, some worry or joy, in the place of Jesus Christ? I know of people and communities which have made a substitution of a secondary for a primary value without really being aware of what they are doing. I see this tendency in my own life too. In my work as a pastor, it is particularly easy to put the church in the place of the true hub. And the Christian church as the center is destructive and unhealthy for those who love it, because it was meant to be the rim, not the hub. We ask too much of a rim when we make it a hub. As the rim it does very well; as the hub it crumples under the weight and pressure.

This shift of center may occur in very subtle ways, so that such weighty and good concerns as vision for church renewal, social justice, evangelism, or personal fulfillment may become in fact the working center of the church, in the place of the wholeness of a biblical center. When this happens, a drying out begins inevitably to take place; the wheel goes eccentric; spokes break off. The church loses its sense of its own frailty, and with that its sense of humor; it takes itself too seriously. At last, as the afternoon wears on, the church grows weary. The warm, friendly, personal center is replaced by a special concern, an idea, or a program. God never intended either ideas or ideals to be the center of our life in the world. The true center is his living decision by which he made the world and redeemed the world, and by which he sustains the world until the time of his fulfillment of the world. That living decision is Jesus Christ the Lord.

At this establishment of beginnings it is of vital importance that we who are Christians are clear about the hub and the rim and the spokes, if we ourselves are to avoid the shift toward the edge, and if we are to play our part in helping those who have gone stale in the afternoon to find their way to nourishment and health. This means that staying fresh ourselves is the first cure. If you don't want to catch a cold, then stay healthy! C. S. Lewis pointed out that "the best safeguard against bad literature is a full experience of good; just as a real and affectionate acquaintance with honest people gives a better protection against rogues than a habitual distrust of everyone."[1] The same is true about keeping on center in our faith.

It's important to keep our families healthy, too! The drift toward the edge starts early for most people. It may start soon after a person is born. What I mean is that there are homes that are precultic homes. They are like training centers in which children are prepared for the airport and street recruiters that are active near every university and college. And some of these precultic homes are Christian homes, but they are also homes in which something has set in motion a process of adriftness. Values are not clarified and shared, or the values that are shared have little nourishment in them.

There are ways to test for adriftness in a family, and each of us should take the test. Table talk at dinner is one such test of the attitude and world-view of the home. Is there despair and pessimism just beneath the surface as the family members talk among themselves? "The school is going down the drain; this city is unfit to live in any more; the crooks in Wall Street have us by the neck; the President is soft on communism; the preacher is spineless . . . the choir is way too loud . . . did you notice that the neighbors don't keep up their yard? And how was your day at Sunday School, Jane?" When the adriftness sets in, the fundamental premises are pessimism and fear and anger. A child in such a home learns of a hopeless future, of a world gone so bad that even Jesus Christ himself is not strong enough to do anything about it. The training is not a training in realism. It is a training in fear, and it is not surprising that, apart from the grace of God, such a child is being prepared for the cultisms of escapism, of fanaticism, or of survivalism. This child may never have been physically beaten, yet, nevertheless, such a boy or girl has been spiritually and emotionally battered.

But there is also the adriftness of optimism. There are precultic families which allow nothing negative as family tabletalk, which reject sinfulness and its ambiguities, which postpone or avoid all realistic discussion by a magic wand of "positive" but meaningless affirmation. This too is a dangerous school of life for children and adults, because in place of the real gospel of forgiveness and healing, from which comes hope, there has been substitited the false gospel of, "We are all the beautiful people who need nothing."

What families need is the nourishing realism of the true gospel, where human failure and complexity can be faced head on. The family which believes in and tries out the power of forgiveness in relationship with each other learns about forgiveness firsthand, and therefore finds it very hard to face the world with fear. If there is no lost cause in our family, then there is no lost cause in the world. It was the practical effect of the love of Christ that taught me this truth. Families need to know how to weep, because of the real sorrows of human suffering, and to break into spontaneous laughter, because of the sheer goodness of being alive and being together.

The journey toward a balanced discipleship begins at this beginning. This is why our family experiences and relationships are so important. We must always be asking the spoke, rim, and hub questions about our own families. And as a family we need not only to talk together, but to experience life together. Our children need adventures in order to learn about risk-taking, which prepares the human personality for faith and love and hope. Go climb a mountain with your kids! Plan a trip, work a one-thousand-piece puzzle together during the rainy season, build block towers as tall as Dad, read aloud the stories of good catastrophes, talk together about faith and hope and love, break all the bedtime rules and go out for ice cream some evening, and then do each of these adventures again and again, so that they become traditions. What have you done when you do this? You have stirred up the spokes and strengthened the rim, and as your children listen to and watch your life unfold they will be drawn to Jesus Christ, the good Convergence Point who is your hub.

To keep from getting a cold don't catch a cold. Stay healthy to be healthy. And all of the ingredients that *keep* us healthy will also restore us when sickness strikes. Prayer as a daily, specific, thoughtful experience keeps us well. Bible study that draws us into the text so that we really hear it keeps us well. Stewardship that acknowledges the reign of Christ over our lives by the regular and generous sharing of our gifts and resources keeps our priorities clear. Concern for real people in real places because of Christ's love keeps us exercised in grace. We cannot stay in robust health alone. I need the rim—not only my family in our house, but the forever family that is the church.

13.

A STRATEGY FOR
THE WHEEL

It is not an easy task to reestablish the balance of a wheel that is off-center, or to repair a rim that has been cracked or broken by the rivalry and animosity of false doctrines. But here I want to propose a strategy for the repair of an eccentric or broken wheel. The strategy begins at the center, which was our concern in chapter 12, and it continues with the question: How shall we be helpful to individuals who have been drawn away from the true hub toward false hubs? I mean helpfulness in the fullest sense of the word—moral, spiritual, intellectual, physical. There is also a second question: How do we actively relate to the movements themselves that have grown up around the false hubs? Let us consider four principles:

(1) I believe it is important for Christians to think through the various challenges to evangelical faith that these movements pose in a study-teaching context that is as free from exaggeration and overstatement as possible. When a movement with which we Christians have sharp disagreement is under study, it is very important that the theology of that movement be clearly understood. (At the same time, it is equally important to see the *dangers* posed in the movements for what they are without understate-

ment.) An exaggerated description of a false movement and its practices is not helpful for our own protection from error; neither will it make it possible for us to draw the people in the false movement toward the authentic center. If they feel that we have misunderstood their own arguments or that we have treated a secondary point in their doctrine as if it were a central point, then they will indeed find a reason to avoid dialogue which could really be helpful.

The accuracy task is not a simple one, however, because most ideological movements are themselves in flux and are continually changing and redefining their own doctrines. One fortunate development in the last few years has been the increase in the amount of thoughtful study and research that evangelical scholars have directed toward the twentieth-century religious scene.[1] The result of these studies is that we now have available for study the documents of the various movements and the theological evaluation of the movements by Christian scholars.

The Christian who is confronted by a particular group is not empty-handed if, on the one hand, he or she is established in a warm, growing relationship to Jesus Christ and, on the other, he or she is able to be accurately informed about that group by the theological evaluation of informed Christian scholars. There is no substitution for this twofold equipping of the Christian. No amount of angry confrontations at the front door or swift pushaways at airports can equal the basic equipment of the saints—first, knowing Christ personally and, second, being equipped with accurate information.

(2) The second principle is the *wisdom principle*. Wisdom is a highly prized biblical virtue that is ascribed to the person who has the feel of truth as well as the knowledge of truth. The wise man or woman is aware of the whole of reality, and since it takes time for such a virtue to mature we usually find that wisdom is a gift found more often in

an older, more experienced person. Wisdom is very essential if our goal is to rebalance a wheel gone eccentric. It takes the larger-perspective skills of wisdom to draw in loosened spokes and to reestablish them with the true hub without harming either the integrity of the spoke or the integrity of the rim. It takes timing, skill, and the wisdom of love to know how to relate to the dogmatic arrogance and absolute claims that often go along with false hubs.

The wisdom principle remembers that movements and people are all different. For this reason, I do not like to see books on cults that gather together in one volume the various movements of a particular time as if each was the same as the others. Each religious movement deserves its own separate theological critique and discussion without the suggestion that it is just like all the other movements. For this reason I try to resist the title, "cult," as a covering term to describe religious or quasi-religious movements with which I disagree. I would rather refer to them as religious movements, and then seek to understand them and evaluate them theologically in terms of their relationship to the authority and centrality of the biblical norm. Are the doctrines derived from the biblical witness to Jesus Christ? Are the doctrines and the way of life under the check and balance of the biblical witness, or is the movement independent of that testable standard?

It is important to remember that movements are made up of people. How do we relate to the people with wisdom? First, it is a good idea not to freeze a person into a tightly defined category and then not allow them to move. I have seen how damaging it can be when a person is heard to say or express a particular view at one time in his or her life and then is continually reminded of that stated conclusion and not permitted to grow beyond it. Wisdom keeps the doors open, and stays in as close as possible—yet with integrity.

I have discovered in my own experience that very often

a person will begin a long, spiritual-intellectual journey at doorways and way stations that are in themselves partial or even false, but that those movements nevertheless play a certain part in a whole journey. For this reason, it is important in relating to any person to always ask the pastoral question, "What way is this person moving?" Christian faith is a dynamic experience and journey. A historical feature of cultism is that it never welcomes the journeying spirit. In contrast, this alive, journeying spirit has always been the mark of Christian faith. The Christian church in the Book of Acts was first described as people of *the way* (Acts 9). The gospel is not afraid of the inquisitive mind, because the gospel is committed to truth, and truth has always set the whole person free: "You will know the truth, and the truth will make you free" (John 8:32). The wisdom principle takes this teaching about truth and the liberating truth of the gospel with full seriousness. This truth commitment is the underlying foundation of wisdom in the biblical sense.

(3) The third principle is an ethical one. The Christian strategy must itself avoid the shortcut methods that it deplores in false-centered movements. The acts which the Christian does in the name of Christ must be under the lordship of Christ; the Lord whom we serve is also the Lord of our service. This principle establishes a very important limitation that every Christian strategy must obey or else come under the judgment of God. For the Christian there can never be a shortcut ethics which is able to argue that good ends justify corrupt means. Our Lord made the principle clear in the Sermon on the Mount: "Not everyone who says to me, 'Lord, Lord,' shall enter the kingdom of heaven, but he who does the will of my Father..." (Matt. 7:21).

A theoretical idealist may be able to justify the violence against one person's rights if that violence results in a benefit to the social whole. But Jesus Christ has identified himself with all people, whoever those people may be, and because of this great fact, we who name the name of Jesus Christ are bound by *his* logic, which calls us to pray for and love our enemies. The enemy deserves our love because of the cross of Jesus Christ. At Calvary our Lord took the place of every enemy. The ethical implications of this event are very far-reaching. It means that we are to see every other human being through the mediation of Jesus Christ. Their worth is already sealed by the act of Christ. Though our neighbor may be in rebellion against that love, nevertheless, we who are Christians are still to honor all people because of the Redeemer's act.

This does not mean that all people are automatically redeemed by the mighty act of Christ in their behalf. The love of Christ does not erase the freedom of the human personality; therefore, without faith there is no salvation. What I am describing is the universal ethical responsibility that the Christian has because of the act of Christ's redemption in behalf of all of humanity. When we abide by this ethical restraint, we may find the going slower, because we are deprived by our Lord of the apparently speedy solutions that come with ethical shortcuts. But the strategy of the gospel is still stronger than shortcut solutions, because it has the power of the gospel at the heart of it.

This restraint does not mean that there should not be discipline within the church. The Corinthian letters are especially instructive in this regard. Paul *does* advocate that the Christians at Corinth practice discipline within the fellowship. Where there is blatant sinfulness, Paul advocates stern discipline that includes excommunication for the sake of the integrity of the gospel and also the redemptive good of the persons involved:

It is actually reported that there is immorality among you, and of a kind that is not found even among pagans; for a man is living with his father's wife. And you are arrogant!

Ought you not rather to mourn? Let him who has done this be removed from among you (1 Cor. 5:1-2).

Your boasting is not good. Do you not know that a little leaven leavens the whole lump? Cleanse out the old leaven that you may be a new lump, as you really are unleavened. For Christ, our paschal lamb, has been sacrificed. Let us, therefore, celebrate the festival, not with the old leaven, the leaven of malice and evil, but with the unleavened bread of sincerity and truth. I wrote to you in my letter not to associate with immoral men; not at all meaning the immoral of this world, or the greedy and robbers, or idolaters, since then you would need to go out of the world. But rather I wrote to you not to associate with any one who bears the name of brother if he is guilty of immorality or greed, or is an idolater, reviler, drunkard, or robber—not even to eat with such a one. For what have I to do with judging outsiders? Is it not those inside the church whom you are to judge? God judges those outside. "Drive out the wicked person from among you" (1 Cor. 5:6-13).

The evidence of the letters leads us to conclude that the Christians at Corinth took the counsel of Paul seriously, and that they did in fact excommunicate the offending members of the church. Therefore, Paul enlarges the pastoral counsel of his first letter by the counsel of the second letter:

For I made up my mind not to make you another painful visit. For if I cause you pain, who is there to make me glad but the one whom I have pained? And I wrote as I did, so that I might not suffer pain from those who should have made me rejoice, for I felt sure of all of you, that my joy would be the joy of you all. For I wrote you out of much affliction and anguish of heart and with many tears, not to cause you pain but to let you know the abundant love that I have for you.

But if any one has caused pain, he has caused it not to me, but in some measure—not to put it too severely—to you all. For such a one this punishment by the majority is enough; so you should rather turn to forgive and comfort him, or he may be overwhelmed by excessive sorrow. So I beg you to reaffirm your love for him. For this is why I wrote, that I might test you and know whether you are obedient in everything. Any one whom you forgive, I also forgive. What I have forgiven, if I have forgiven anything, has been for your sake in the presence of Christ, to keep Satan from gaining the advantage over us; for we are not ignorant of his designs (2 Cor. 2:1–11).

Taken together, these texts give to us the context within which discipline may be exercised helpfully in the church.

(4) The fourth principle I will call the strategy of the thousand single steps. Another way of putting this principle is to describe it as the principle of the long view. Take the long view in all human relationships. Relate to every person you meet as if you will know that person all your life. Such a perspective upgrades each relationship, even those countless encounters that never extend beyond the day or a few moments. When it comes to the sometimes very painful dialogues with family members or close friends who have become entangled in false movements, the long-view approach puts each discussion into a larger framework. It means that everything does not depend upon the words we are able to put together in any particular conversation; rather the chief responsibility we have is to be faithful within one part of a larger whole. Even my own misstatements or mistakes may later play a part in the whole spiritual journey of my friend.

In other words, this principle recognizes the theological fact that I am not the convincer or the converter; it is the Holy Spirit who must authenticate every witness to the gospel, and it is the Holy Spirit who confirms the total collection of parts so that a person is able to find the true pathway.

We who are Christians have responsibility to bear witness to our faith, but we have limited responsibility. It is God himself who is the ultimate evangelist and apologist for the gospel; we are not burdened with that responsibility. I believe that we function better as witnesses, whether in an evangelistic situation, an apologetic situation, or a church discipline situation, when we do not take onto ourselves more responsibility than God has granted to us.

We do not have the task of telling the whole story to anyone, but we do have the task of being an authentic, single influence—of saying perhaps a few important things. Add these together with the mistakes we make, both in words and acts, and you have a picture of what Christian witness is all about. But the mystery of the Holy Spirit is that God makes use of these partial ingredients, incomplete and faulty as they are, to fit in with the total mixture of influences he uses to confirm the worthiness of the claims of Jesus Christ to a human being. The strategy of the long view trusts in the Lord to be his own best proof, and this principle recognizes that all of this usually takes time.

The cure for imbalance is always getting back in touch with the center. Christian faith is first of all a relationship with Jesus Christ. It is the sheer immensity of that good Convergence Point that wins us to faith. What we must never do is to scale down its claim or its inner integrity in some endeavor either to make the gospel "more relevant" or to recapture some person we care about who may have drifted away from its warmth and light. Jesus Christ is trustworthy to be the hub of our existence. He has the strength to hold the wheel in balance and enable it to function properly. Our task is to faithfully live with Jesus Christ, the enormous Exception, as center.

I have not minimized the scale of the miracle, as some of our milder theologians think it wise to do. Rather have I deliberately dwelt on that incredible interruption, as a blow that broke the very backbone of history. I have great sympathy with the monotheists. Those in Islam and Judaism to whom it seems a blasphemy; a blasphemy that might shake the world. But it did not shake the world; it steadied the world.[1]

NOTES

Introduction
1. Dorothy L. Sayers, *Christian Letters to a Post-Christian World* (Grand Rapids, Mich.: Wm. B. Eerdmans Publishing Co., 1967), p. 139.
2. Clive S. Lewis, *The Screwtape Letters*, bound with "Screwtape Proposes a Toast" (New York: Macmillan Publishing Co., 1961), p. 154.

Chapter 1
1. See J. R. R. Tolkein's chapter, "On Fairy Tales," in C. S. Lewis, ed., *Essays Presented to Charles Williams* (Grand Rapids, Mich.: Wm. B. Eerdmans Publishing Co., 1966).

Chapter 3
1. Dietrich Bonhoeffer, *Letters and Papers from Prison*, rev. and enlarged ed., ed. Eberhard Bethge (New York: Macmillan Publishing Co., 1972), p. 157.
2. See Bonhoeffer, *The Cost of Discipleship* (London: SCM Press, 1964), p. 35.
3. John Bunyan, *The Pilgrim's Progress*, rev. ed. (New York: E. P. Dutton & Co., 1954), p. 253.
4. Clive S. Lewis, *Surprised by Joy: The Shape of My Early Life* (New York: Harcourt Brace & World, Harvest Books, 1955), p. 230.

Chapter 4
1. C. S. Lewis, *Miracles: A Preliminary Study* (London: Geoffrey Bles; New York: Macmillan Publishing Co., 1947), p. 133.

Chapter 5
1. Karl Barth, *Dogmatics in Outline* (New York: Harper & Row, Publisher, 1959), p. 152.

Chapter 7
1. G. K. Chesterton, *Orthodoxy* (New York: Doubleday & Co., Image Books, 1969), p. 100.
2. Karl Barth, "Testing of Doctrine," *Dogmatics in Outline* (New York: Harper & Row, Pubs., Torch Books, 1959), pp. 12, 13.

Chapter 8
1. Quoted from *The Book of Confessions* of the United Presbyterian Church, U.S.A., 2nd ed., 1970.
2. Aleksandr Solzhenitsyn, *The Gulag Archipelago 1918–1956: An Experiment in Literary Investigation*, tr. Thomas P. Whitney (New York: Harper & Row Pubs., 1974), pp. 27–28.

Chapter 10
1. Quoted in *Early Church Fathers*, ed. Cyril C. Richardson (New York: Macmillan Publishing Co., 1970), p. 358.
2. Frederick Dale Bruner, *A Theology of the Holy Spirit: The Pentecostal Experience and the New Testament Witness* (New York: Wm. B. Eerdmans Publishing Co., 1970), pp. 318, 319.
3. Richard Bach, *Jonathan Livingston Seagull* (New York: Macmillan Publishing Co., 1970).
4. Quoted from *The Book of Common Prayer* (New York: Seabury Press, 1976), pp. 237–238.
5. Quoted in *Early Church Fathers*, ed. Richardson, p. 379.

Chapter 11
1. G. K. Chesterton, *Orthodoxy* (New York: Doubleday & Co., Image Books, 1959), p. 72.
2. E. F. Palmer, *1, 2, 3 John, Revelation*, The Communicator's Commentary, vol. 12 (Waco, Tex., Word Books, 1982).
3. C. S. Lewis, *The Screwtape Letters*, bound with "Screwtape Proposes a Toast" (New York: Macmillan Publishing Co., 1961).

Chapter 12

1. C. S. Lewis, *Experiment in Criticism* (New York: Cambridge Univ. Press, 1961), p. 94.

Chapter 13

1. For example, the studies that are available through the research of the Spiritual Counterfeits Project in Berkeley.